# ENLIGHTENED A PARENT'S GUIDE IN AI EDUCATION

*How to Prepare Yourself and Your Family for the Future of Technology*

Anant

# Table of Contents

# DEDICATION

Anant is an immersive experience that will impact your heart and mind because of the author's.

Skillful blend of compelling storytelling, helpful advice, and viewpoints.

Their writings are meant to encourage readers to lead purposeful lives, seek out opportunities for self-improvement, and help create a world where spiritual enlightenment and technological progress can coexist fully in the future.

Learn and grow alongside Anant on this life-altering expedition. Explore a wealth of materials, learn about forthcoming releases, and have thought-provoking discussions by following them on social media and visiting their online website. **https://enlightenedanant.com**

Open your mind to new ideas and experiences and accept the intimate knowledge you already possess.

At last, a moving tribute to the boundless potential in every child I hope this book serves as a light to help them discover the joy of studying, foster a lifelong love of knowledge, and discover and develop their intrinsic capacity to build a future in which AI is used to benefit humanity.

Thank you very much.

Anant

# ABOUT THE AUTHOR

Anant is an unwavering advocate of learning, development, and the transformational potential of information. Anant has devoted every day to helping others achieve their full potential by sharing their profound knowledge of the human mind and unyielding dedication to enlightenment.

The authors of Enlightened Anant draw on a wide range of experience in the field of education, psychology, and spirituality to create a tapestry of wisdom, insight, and inspiration in their writings. Anant's approach to self-exploration and development is one of a kind; it combines in-depth introspection with study and an intuitive grasp of the human experience.

The topics covered in Anant's works range from self-help and self-improvement to spirituality and the incorporation of AI in the classroom. Each book embodies their unyielding faith in the power of the human mind and the wisdom that lies dormant within each of us.

Reading Anant is an immersive experience that will impact your heart and mind because of the author's skillful blend of compelling storytelling, helpful advice, and unique view points. The writings are meant to encourage readers to lead purposeful lives, seek out opportunities for self-improvement, and help create a world where spiritual enlightenment and technological progress can coexist peacefully in the future.

Learn and grow alongside Anant on this life-altering expedition. Explore a wealth of materials; learn about forthcoming releases, and have thought-provoking discussions by following them on social media and visiting their official website. **https://enlightenedanant.com**

Open your mind to new ideas and experiences and accept the immense knowledge you already possess.

# FORWORD

As a society, we stand on the precipice of an incredible revolution. Artificial Intelligence, or AI, has emerged as a powerful force that has the potential to shape our future in ways, we never idea possible. It has already begun transforming industries, revolutionizing the way we live, paintings, and interacting with the world round us.

In the midst of this revolution, we find ourselves entrusted with a profound responsibility - nurturing the potential of our children. As parents, educators, and caretakers, we play a pivotal role in guiding our children via a global where AI has become an integral part of daily life.

"Enlightened: A Parent's Guide in AI Education; A Practical Parent's Guide to AI and the Future in the Digital World," is a timely and invaluable resource that equips us with the knowledge, insights, and practical strategies that we need to navigate this ever-evolving landscape. This ebook is a guiding mild, illuminating the path ahead and empowering us to embrace the potential of AI while ensuring the best possible future for our children.

Authored with expertise and a deep understanding of the subject matter, **"Unlocking Your Child's Potential"** unravels the complexities of AI in a friendly and accessible manner. It goes beyond just explaining the technical aspects of AI and delves into its profound impact on diverse facets of our children's lives - from education to personal increase, from career opportunities to ethical considerations.

What sets this e book apart is its emphasis on practicality. It offers concrete strategies and actionable advice for parents to foster their toddler's development in a world driven by using AI. From cultivating critical questioning abilities to nurturing creativity and empathy, this guide provides invaluable gear to help our children thrive in an AI-driven future.

Through engaging narratives, expert evaluation, and real-global examples, we gain a comprehensive understanding of AI's potential to unencumbered our children's capabilities. We learn how AI can personalize education; enhance problem-fixing abilities, and open doors to new possibilities. Furthermore, the book encourages us to explore the ethical dimensions of AI, guiding us in elevating responsible digital citizens who understand the broader impact of their actions.

As we embark on this journey, we are reminded that technology alone isn't the answer. It is the combination of human ingenuity, compassion, and adaptability so that it will absolutely empower our children to navigate the challenges and seize the opportunities presented by AI.

I invite you to immerse yourself in the pages of "Unlocking Your Child's Potential" and discover the transformative power of AI. Let us embrace this revolution with open minds, preparing ourselves and our children for a future complete of promise. Together, we can unlock a world of possibilities and empower our children to thrive in the virtual globe.

[Forward Anant]

"AI is not our enemy; it is our companion. It can empower us, augment our capabilities, and unlock new possibilities for our children's future." - Sundar Pichai

"The best way to predict the future is to create it. Let's embrace AI as a means to shape a brighter future for our children." - Andrew Ng

# WHAT WILL WE LEARN?

In this book, we will embark on an exciting journey into the world of artificial intelligence (AI) and its profound impact on our lives, particularly in the context of preparing ourselves and our families for the future. Through a comprehensive exploration of various topics and applications, we will delve into the transformative potential of AI in education, parenting, personal growth, and beyond.

- ❖ **The Fundamentals of Ai:** We will start by understanding what AI is, its historical evolution, and the current state of AI applications. By exploring its significance and widespread use, we will develop a solid foundation to comprehend its implications in our lives.

- ❖ **AI in Education and Parenting:** We will discover how AI can revolutionize the way we educate our children and support their growth. From personalized learning to cognitive development, we will explore the benefits, challenges, and opportunities AI presents in nurturing digital intelligence and inspiring creativity.

- ❖ **Ensuring Safety and Well-Being:** AI plays a crucial role in safeguarding our children in the digital age. We will explore how AI enhances monitoring, ensures online and offline safety, and supports children's mental health and well-being. Strategies for maintaining a healthy balance with technology will also be discussed.

- ❖ **Ethical Considerations and Future Perspectives:** As we delve into the world of AI, we will navigate the ethical considerations surrounding its use. We will explore the importance of critical thinking, privacy, and responsible decision-making in an AI-driven era. Furthermore, we will explore career opportunities in AI and guide children towards success in this rapidly evolving field.

- ❖ **Practical Applications and Tools:** This book will provide practical guidance on integrating AI technology into our daily lives. From harnessing AI for productivity and convenience to supporting children's learning and development, we will explore how AI can be utilized to its fullest potential.

- ❖ **Nurturing Future-Ready Minds:** Explore the qualities and skills needed for success in a future shaped by AI. Learn how to cultivate critical thinking, adaptability, creativity, empathy, and collaboration in your child, empowering them to thrive in a rapidly changing world. By the end of this book, readers will have a deep understanding of AI and its implications for education, parenting, personal growth, and the future. They will be equipped with valuable insights, practical strategies, and ethical considerations to navigate the Unlocking Your Child's Potential and embrace its benefits while fostering empathy, compassion, and privacy values in their families. Together, let's embark on this transformative journey and prepare ourselves and our loved ones for the AI revolution. Enlightened A parent's Guide in AI Education is your essential guide to preparing your child for a future where AI plays a central role, ensuring they can navigate the challenges and embrace the opportunities that lie ahead.

# SECTION 1

# THE FUNDAMENTALS OF AI

# INTRODUCTION

Welcome to Enlightened A parent'sGuide in AI Education

In this book, we embark on an exciting journey together, exploring the incredible possibilities that lie ahead for our children in the age of AI. As a parent, you play a crucial role in shaping your child's future, and it's essential to understand how artificial intelligence is transforming our world and how you can prepare your child for success.

The rapid advancement of AI has brought about significant changes in various aspects of our lives, from education to work and everything in between. It has become imperative for us to embrace this new reality and quip ourselves with the knowledge and tools to navigate the evolving landscape.

But don't worry, this book is here to guide you every step of the way! Written with a friendly and accessible tone, we will unravel the mysteries of AI and its impact on our children's potential. You don't need to be an expert in technology; will break down complex concepts into easy-to-understand explanations.

Throughout the pages, you'll find engaging narratives, expert insights, and practical strategies to empower you as a parent. We will explore topics such as personalized learning, digital intelligence, ethical considerations, and so much more. You'll gain a deep understanding of how AI can enhance your child's education, foster their creativity, and prepare them for a future where technological advancements continue to shape the world.

We live in a comprehensive approach to parenting, and that's why we'll explore not just the benefits but also the challenges and ethical considerations associated with AI. By doing so, we can navigate the digital world with confidence and ensure that our children become responsible and ethical uses of AI technologies.

So, join us on this exciting adventure! Together, let's unlock your child's potential, harness the power of AI, and prepare them for a future full of opportunities. Get ready to be inspired, informed, and empowered as we embark on this transformative journey into the world of AI and the digital future.

Let's unlock a world of possibilities for our children!

# THE AI REVOLUTION

The fundamentals of artificial intelligence (AI) have laid a strong foundation, enabling machines to learn, understand language, process visual information, and make intelligent decisions. But what comes next? In this chapter, we'll look into the AI revolution and explore how it is reshaping our world. We'll discuss why it's crucial to embrace this revolution and adopt AI in various domains and industries. Get ready for a glimpse into the future!

- ❖ **The Winds of Change:** The world is undergoing a profound transformation driven by AI. From healthcare and finance to transportation and education, AI is revolutionizing industries, bringing efficiency, innovation, and new possibilities. The impact is far-reaching, altering the way we live, work, and interact. Embracing this change is essential to stay relevant and thrive in the fast-paced, AI-powered landscape.

- ❖ **Unlocking New Opportunities:** Adopting AI opens doors to exciting opportunities. Businesses can leverage AI to enhance productivity, optimize processes, and gain valuable insights from vast amounts of data. Automation and intelligent systems streamline operations, freeing up human resources to focus on creative and strategic endeavors. Startups and entrepreneurs can disrupt traditional models, creating innovative AI-driven solutions that address complex challenges.

- ❖ **Enhancing Decision-Making:** AI empowers decision-makers with intelligent tools that augment their capabilities. Through data analysis and predictive modeling, AI systems provide valuable insights for informed decision-making. From personalized recommendations to risk assessment and strategic planning, AI algorithms process vast data sets, enabling better choices with higher accuracy and efficiency.

❖ **Accelerating Scientific Discovery:** AI is revolutionizing scientific research and exploration. By analyzing massive data sets, AI algorithms help scientists discover patterns, make predictions, and uncover hidden insights. In fields like genomics, climate modeling, and drug discovery, AI accelerates progress by reducing the time and cost required for breakthroughs. It opens up new frontiers, pushing the boundaries of human knowledge.

❖ **Improving Healthcare:** The healthcare industry is experiencing a transformative impact through AI. Intelligent algorithms can aid in disease diagnosis, personalized treatment plans, and drug discovery. AI-enabled devices and wearable monitor patient health, enabling early detection and proactive interventions. With AI, healthcare becomes more precise, accessible, and cost-effective, ultimately saving lives and

❖ **Conclusion:** The AI revolution is underway, and its impact is undeniable. Embracing this transformation is vital for individuals, businesses, and society as a whole. By adopting AI, we unlock new opportunities, enhance decision-making, accelerate scientific progress, revolutionize healthcare, reshape education, and tackle countless challenges. It is through a proactive and responsible approach that we can harness the full potential of AI and create a brighter future for all. So, let's embrace the AI revolution and embark on this transformative journey together.

15

# A BRIEF HISTORY

Let's take a quick trip down memory lane and explore the fascinating history of AI. Don't worry; it won't be a boring history class! We'll keep it short.

AI has been around for quite some time, but it's really gained momentum in recent decades. The roots of AI can be traced back to the mid-20th century when researchers began dreaming of creating machines that could mimic human intelligence.

In the 1950s and 1960s, AI donors started developing the first AI programs and exploring concepts like problem-solving and symbolic reasoning. They were driven by a vision of creating machines that could think and learn like humans. It was an exciting time of experimentation and discovery.

However, as researchers explored deeper, they soon realized that AI was more challenging than they initially thought. Progress was slower than expected, and AI went through what's known as an "AI winter," a period of reduced interest and funding.

The 1980s and 1990s marked a resurgence of AI. Researchers began exploring innovative approaches, such as machine learning and neural networks. These techniques allow AI systems to learn from data and make predictions, opening new possibilities.

Fast forward to the 21st century, and AI has become increasingly prevalent in our lives. We now have virtual assistants like Siri and Alexa, self-driving cars, and recommendation systems that suggest movies or products we might like. AI has truly become a part of our everyday experiences.

On important development that contributed to the progress of AI is the availability of vast amounts of data and increased computing power. This combination has allowed AI systems to train on massive datasets and perform complex tasks more efficiently.

As AI becomes more powerful and integrated into various industries, it's essential to consider its ethical implications. Questions around privacy, bias, and transparency have gained prominence, leading to discussions on responsible AI development and deployment.

So, that's a brief overview of the history of AI in a nutshell! From its early beginnings to its current widespread applications, AI has come a long way. It's an exciting field that holds immense potential for shaping the future.

# WHAT IS AI AND WHY IS IT IMPORTANT?

AI is not just a new piece of technology; it is a game-changer that could change the way we live, work, and raise our children. So, let me spark your interest and encourage you to see how important AI is in your parenting journey.

Imagine a computer that is so smart that it can think, learn, and analyze data just like a human thought. That's all there is to AI. But why is it so important for you as parents to know and understand what it means?

First of all, AI can be your best friend when it comes to automating tedious and time-consuming chorus. Imagine having a personal helper who could take care of the little things so you could spend more time with your kids. It's like getting back valuable time that you can use to strengthen relationships and make memories that really matter.

But AI is more than just machinery. It has a unique ability to look at huge amounts of data, find patterns, and give insights that can lead to important new discoveries. AI works like a detective in fields like medicine, climate science, and education to find hidden information and help us make better decisions. By understanding and using AI, you can help this field move forward and make a better future for your children and future generations.

Another important area where AI shines is personalization. Just think about how Netflix and Spotify give you suggestions based on what you like. AI systems learn what you like, which helps you find content that is really relevant to you. This personalization can also be used in education, so teachers can make lesson plans for each child that is based on how they learn and what they need. By using AI, you can open up a world of personalized experiences for your kids, which will help them develop their interests and keep them interested.

AI is also important because it makes things safer and easier to use. Think about how self-driving cars or smart home devices could make your daily life easier. AI gives us a sense of safety and ads, opens up new possibilities, and gives you the freedom to focus on what really matters: the growth and well-being of your children.

But as we move forward with AI, we must remember how important it is to use it in a responsible and moral way. We need to put things like privacy, fairness, and openness at the top of our list. By making sure people understand those things, we can make sure that AI helps everyone and doesn't leave anyone behind.

Dear parents, if you accept AI, you and your children will have a lot more options. You lead them through a technological landscape that has a lot of potential for their success and happiness in the future. Accepting AI means adjusting to a world that is always changing and giving your kids the skills and knowledge; they need to do well in a world run by AI.

So, let's start out on this amazing trip together. Let's encourage a sense of wonder, learn with our kids, and look into the amazing possibilities that AI brings. By embracing AI as parents, we help our kids' become creators, thinkers, and leaders who make the future better for everyone.

Remember that in the world of AI, there are a lot of different things that could happen, and there is a lot of room for growth and discovery. Accept it, use its power, and let's go out into a world where AI and being a parent work together to create a future with a lot of options.

Let the adventure with AI start!

# UNVEILING THE MAGIC:

Ah, how AI systems work on the inside! Let's take a look at the intriguing world of AI and find out some of the secrets that make it work so well.

AI is based on techniques, which are like a set of instructions for how to do a particular job on a computer. AI systems are made up of these programs, which determine how they learn, think, and make decisions.

Machine learning is one of AI's most important ideas. Here is where the magic takes place! Algorithms for machine learning let computers learn from data and get better over time without being told to do so. They learn patterns, make predictions, and make decisions based on the examples they have been taught.

There are many different kinds of machine learning techniques, but let's focus on two main ones: supervised learning and unsupervised learning.

Using learned data, supervised learning trains an AI system. Imagine showing a computer how to tell the difference between different kinds of fruit. You'd show it pictures of apples, oranges, and bananas and tell it what each one was. The AI would learn to find patterns in the data and then use that knowledge to describe new images of fruits that have not been labeled.

In unsupervised learning, on the other hand, an AI system learns from data that hasn't been learned. It's like giving the computer a bunch of puzzle pieces that are all mixed up and telling it to find patterns or group puzzles that are similar. The program learns to find hidden structures or relationships in the data without any labels that tell it what to look for.

Once an AI system has been taught to use these methods, it can use new data to make predictions or decisions. The word for this is "inference." For example, a trained AI model could look at medical images to help doctors figure out what's wrong with a patient, or it could look at data about customers to figure out what they like and make personalized suggestions.

But AI isn't done being magical yet! There are also more advanced methods, such as deep learning, which uses neural networks based on the way the human brain is built. Deep learning has made it possible for advancements to be made in areas like speech and image recognition.

There are, of course, some things that AI programs can't do. They depend a lot on the quality and amount of data they are trained on, and sometimes they can be biased or make mistakes. Because of this, it's important to have human oversight and think about ethics when making and using AI systems.

Now that we've talked about how AI algorithms work and what they do to power AI systems, it's time to talk about where AI apps are right now. AI's uses in the real world are mind-blowing, believe me!

# AI APPLICATIONS IN EVERYDAY LIFE:

**Uses Of AI In Everyday Life: AI Is Changing Many Parts Of The World.**

The most common uses of AI are:

## Virtual Helpers

- Voice detection is done by Alexa from Amazon, Siri from Apple, and Google Assistant.
- You can use Alexa to set reminders, answer questions, play music, control smart home devices, and get custom suggestions.

## Recommender System

- Education, sports, and social media all use recommendation systems.
- Based on the user's tastes, browsing history, and behavior, AI algorithms suggest items, movies, music, and social connections.

## Autonomous Vehicles

- AI is used to make cars that can drive themselves.
- AVs can navigate and make choices with the help of sensors, cameras, and machine learning algorithms. This makes them safer, more efficient, and reduces the number of accidents.

## Healthcare

- AI is helping doctors find better ways to diagnose, treat, and find new medicines.
- AI programs can look at X-rays and MRIs to find cancer.
- Patients can be triaged, evaluated, and given advice by chat bots.

## Finance

- AI is used in finance to find fraud, evaluate risks, and do algorithmic trading.
- Large financial records are analyzed by machine learning algorithms to find trends, outliers, and risks.

## Logistics and Moving Things

- Logistics and shipping are made better by AI.
- Algorithms that plan routes save time and gas.
- Predictive maintenance systems that use AI can predict when machines will break down and plan for repairs.

## Education

- AI makes learning better and easier to customize.
- In adaptive learning platforms, AI algorithms look at how well a student is doing and suggest material.
- Intelligent teaching tools help and give feedback to each student in their own way.

## AI's Effects on Business:

## Healthcare

- AI helps doctors find problems, analyze images, and give more accurate care.
- EHRs that are backed by AI make it easier to do paperwork and make decisions based on data.

## Finance

- AI makes it easier to spot frauds, help customers, and plan investments.
- AI robots can help with simple banking tasks and financial advice.

## Transportation

- AI makes self-driving cars safer and helps traffic move faster.
- AI-based predictive maintenance is the best way to take care of a vehicle and cuts breakdowns.

## Education

- AI helps with individualized learning, adaptive tasks, and smart coaching.
- With tools that are driven by AI, administrators can focus on teaching and helping.

## When You Shop Online

- AI makes it possible to make personalized recommendations for products, predict demand, and keep track of stock.
- Chat bots make shopping, sales, and customer service better.

## Manufacturing

- Automation that is driven by AI improves production, quality, and downtime.
- Predictive maintenance cuts down on equipment failures and makes sure that maintenance plans work best.

These examples show how AI is changing businesses and making them more efficient, better at making decisions, and more open to new ideas. Parents need to understand how AI works so they can prepare their kids for a world with AI.

# SECTION 2

# AI EDUCATION AND PARENTING

# AI IN EDUCATION

Automatic Systems for Learning Making kids' lives better through learning environments and giving parents more power.

Families can use educational resources that are provided by artificial intelligence to add to and improve their children's education. The following are some methods:

- ❖ **One-on-One Instruction:** Artificial intelligence can be used to make educational resources that fit different learning styles, strategies, and preferences. Parents can use these tools to make personalized lessons for their kids, which makes it more likely that their kids will fully understand complicated ideas.

- ❖ **Flexible Assessment:** Assessment tools that are powered by artificial intelligence can look at how well a child is doing, find his or her strengths and weaknesses, and give the child personalized help. Families can use this knowledge to guide their child's education and focus on areas where the child is weak.

- ❖ **Intelligent Education Systems:** AI-based education systems let you learn in a way that is interactive and flexible. Students can get immediate feedback, explanations, and help from these systems, which makes it easier for them to understand tough ideas.

- ❖ **Enhanced Engagement:** Most educational resources that are powered by AI have interactive parts, can be turned into games, and provide immersive experiences. Families can use these features to make learning more fun and interesting, which will spark their child's interest and motivate them to work hard.

- ❖ **A Variety of Content:** AI programs can use a child's interests and learning goals to find and recommend educational content. Families can use AI-powered platforms to get access to a wide range of high-quality educational resources, such as interactive videos, games, and virtual reality (VR) experiences.

- ❖ **Language Learning and Text Translation:** AI-powered apps and translation tools can help kids learn new languages, expand their knowledge, and connect with people from all walks of life.

Children can use systems that use artificial intelligence (AI) to make things like essays, presentations, and art. Families can use these tools to help their kids get better at expressing themselves creatively and making their work better.

- ❖ **Together, We Can Learn:** Students can work on projects together, share ideas, and give and get feedback from their peers when they use AI-powered tools. Families can help their kids by getting them involved in cooperative learning activities made possible by artificial intelligence technologies.

- ❖ **Insights Data to back it Up:** Artificial intelligence (AI)-powered educational resources collect and analyze data about a student's performance, study habits, and interests. Families can use this knowledge to talk to teachers better, keep track of their child's progress, and make smart decisions about their child's education.

❖ **Helping Students Learn Around the Clock:** Material that has been improved with AI can be used to help students study outside of class. Families can encourage their kids to use these tools to do research and learn more about things that interest them on their own. Using AI-powered educational resources, families can add to traditional teaching methods, tailor lessons to their children's needs, and improve their children's learning environments through interactive, personalized methods.

# PREPARING CHILDREN A PARENTS FOR A WORLD OF POSSIBILITIES

Hey, parents and kids need to be taught, made aware of, and helped to improve their critical thinking skills so they are ready for the exciting AI change. You can help them get used to their new home by doing some fun things, such as:

**Let's Look More Closely At STEM Education:** STEM means science, technology, engineering, and math. By starting with these topics, you can learn a lot about AI and the great ideas that go into it. AI is something kids can learn a lot about in school and at fun programs that offer STEM classes outside of school.

 **The Key Is Digital Literacy:** teaching kids how to use technology well and safely so they can become digital whizzes. We are talking about how to be a good digital citizen, how to stay safe online, and how to evaluate information sources. If you teach them how to think critically, they will be able to figure out whether AI-driven systems are telling the truth or if they are biased.

Let your creativity and sense of wonder show. Tell kids to be creative and interested. Encourage them to try AI tools such as computers, robots, apps, and games. This will get them excited, help them figure out how to fix problems better, and teach them more about AI.

Ethics are something you should think about. Talk about the moral effects of AI from your heart. Let's try to use technology in a way that is fair, honest, and smart. Encourage kids to think about how AI affects society, how it affects privacy, and how it might be biased.

**The Goal Is To Keep Learning All Your Life:** Help parents and kids see that learning about artificial intelligence is a fun journey that never ends. Tell them to keep up with the latest AI (artificial intelligence) developments and uses. They can take classes, webinars, or online courses that focus on artificial intelligence and other related subjects.

Power to Change is impressive, and so is working together. Remind everyone that in an AI-run world, it's very important to work as a team and be able to adapt. Encourage kids to work together, fix problems as a group, and learn important social skills as well as technical ones. AI works with people most of the time, so these skills will be helpful.

Let's combine AI with morality by encouraging kids with a strong sense of right and wrong to go into AI and similar fields. Ask them to think about how they could help make AI systems that are fair, include everyone, and help society. They have the power to change things for the better.

Remember that the AI revolution has opened a lot of great choices, and that preparing the children and the parents for this world, is to give them the tools to understand, adapt to, and shape the future. We can help them learn, think critically, and think about ethics so that they are ready to take advantage of the exciting opportunities that AI offers. First, let's look at AI as a whole.

Are you ready to join the AI revolution and build a world where people and technology work together? Let's find out more about all the fun things that might happen. But first, here are a few things you should know: Why should you care about computers that learn?

# AI IN PARENTING AND EDUCATION

Welcome to the exciting world of artificial intelligence in teaching and schooling! In this part, we'll look at how AI is changing how we teach and raise our kids. I got ready to find out about all the cool things that AI can do.

Technologies that use AI are changing how employees do their jobs. AI is giving parents new tools and insights to help them deal with the challenges of raising children. For example, smart baby monitors can track a baby's sleep patterns and let parents know when they wake up. Virtual parenting assistants can give advice and support based on a child's developmental milestones.

Personalized learning is one place where AI really shines in education. AI algorithms can look at a lot of information about a student's learning style, strengths, and weaknesses to make materials and learning experiences that are tailored to each student. Intelligent teaching systems can give feedback and help that is tailored to each student. This makes learning more interesting and efficient. This personalized method lets students learn at their own pace, which makes them more invested in learning and improves their education.

AI is also improving schooling by making learning tools more interactive. AI-powered virtual reality (VR) and Augmented Reality (AR) technologies let students immerse themselves in virtual settings that make learning come to life. AI-enhanced learning experiences offer a whole new level of engagement and understanding, whether it's learning about alternative cultures or dissecting virtual organisms.

AI is also used to teach and grade students. AI-powered automated grading systems can quickly grade assignments and give instant feedback, saving teachers a lot of time. AI can analyze written answers with the help of algorithms for natural language processing. This helps to figure out where students might need more help and input.

AI is making schooling more useful outside of the classroom as well as in the classroom. AI algorithms are used by online learning systems to make personalized curriculum suggestions, adaptive assessments, and smart course suggestions. This makes it possible for students to get a good education from anywhere in the world and at their own pace.

AI has many benefits for teaching and learning, but it's important to think about ethical issues. Protecting the privacy of student data, making sure algorithms are fair, and keeping human eyes open are all important parts of making AI systems that put children's well-being and growth first.

AI has a bright future in teaching and education, and this is an area that keeps changing quickly. As we recognize AI's potential, it's important to find a balance between using technology and nurturing the human connections and sensibilities that are so important in teaching and education.

Are you excited to learn more about how AI can change the way professionals and teachers do their jobs? In the next part, we'll learn more about specific AI applications and look at inspiring examples that are shaping the future of learning. I got ready to be amazed by all the amazing things AI can do for teaching and schooling. Let's continue our AI adventure together!

# IMPORTANCE OF COMPUTERS

**Innovation and Economic Growth:** AI can drive both innovation and economic growth. It makes it easier to come up with new goods, services, and ways to run a business. Companions and industries that use AI can give themselves a competitive edge and help the economy grow.

**Taking on Complex Problems:** Computers that can learn can help people deal with big problems like climate change, health care inequality, and making the best use of resources. AI can help with a lot of things, like studying climate data, making personalized health care solutions, and figuring out how to use energy most efficiently.

**Ethics:** As AI becomes more common, it's important to think about the ethical aspects of how it's used. If you care about computers that can teach, you should take part in talks about how to build AI in a way that is fair, open, accountable, and protects people's privacy. Being aware of and taking part in these talks makes sure that AI technologies are built and used in a way that is ethical and helpful.

**In the end,** worrying about computers that can teach lets us take advantage of the possible benefits of AI while also dealing with the problems and ethical questions that come with it. It gives people the tools they need to shape the future of technology and how it affects society.

# THE CURRENT STATE OF AI APPLICATIONS

AI is tremendously busy and interesting right now, and there are many ways to use it.

We can't wait to get to this part, where we'll look at how AI is used right now. I was ready to be amazed by how AI is changing many businesses and parts of our lives in amazing ways.

The field of health care is making a lot of progress with AI. Medical images, like X-rays and MRIs, can be looked at by systems that use AI. This makes it easier and faster for doctors to find the right diseases. AI systems can also look through huge amounts of data about patients to find patterns and predict possible health risks. This leads to better evaluations, better planning for treatment, and better long-term results for the patient.

In the world of finance, AI is changing how we deal with money. AI systems can look at financial data and search for signs of theft. They can also give real-time estimates. This is a great way for banks and other financial companies to find out about suspicious behavior and stop scams. Also, AI-powered apps and virtual assistants make the customer experience better by giving them personalized advice and helping with their money.

AI is about to change a lot about how people get around. AI-controlled self-driving cars are being built to make roads safer and cut down on traffic. These cars use sensors, cameras, and complicated systems to figure out where they are and what to do next. In the transportation business, AI is helping to improve how the supply chain works, plan routes better, and make delivery methods more efficient.

AI is also changing how medicine is done and how people have fun. AI algorithms are used by streaming services like Netflix and Spotify to give us custom content based on what we like to watch and how often we watch it. This helps us find new movies, TV shows, and songs we'll like. AI is also used to make computer characters for video games that look and act like real people and can respond to what the player does.

In education, AI-powered tools are used to give students unique ways to learn and tests that change depending on how they do them. Even creative fields like music, art, and making content are starting to use AI.

When we look at how AI is used now, it's clear that things are changing quickly. AI can do a lot, and we're just starting to scratch the surface of what it can do. But there's more! After that, we'll talk about the exciting ways AI can help kids and teachers. Find out how AI is affecting the way we teach and raise our children. AI is changing the future of education by making learning more personalized and by making training systems smarter. I was excited to learn a lot about how AI can help teachers and students. Let's keep going on our AI path together!

# THE IMPORTANCE OF AI IN YOUR CHILD'S EDUCATION

My dear parents! Let's look at why artificial intelligence is so important for your child's schooling. Get ready to find out how AI is changing the way kids learn and helping them reach their full potential.

First of all, individual learning changes the way things are done. AI knows that each child is different and learns in a different way. With AI algorithms sifting through data about your child's skills, weaknesses, and learning style, their education can be made to fit their needs. It's like having a personal teacher who knows how to get the best out of your child.

But that's not all! AI helps your child in ways that are best for them. Intelligent tutoring systems that are run by AI work like virtual tutors and give your child instant feedback and help as they learn. If they run into a difficult situation, AI steps in with personalized material and interventions to help them get past the problem and reach their full potential. It's like having a cheering coach there for them all the time.

Imagine your child going on learning trips that are all-encompassing. AI-driven technologies like virtual reality (VR) and Augmented Reality (AR) let people explore, build, and interact with complex ideas in virtual environments. It's like taking them on fun field trips without leaving the classroom! These activities make learning interesting, fun, and memorable.

Another good thing is that AI isn't just used in the classroom. AI-driven online learning systems offer flexible and personalized ways to learn. Whether your child wants to learn new skills, explore their interests, or keep learning for the rest of their lives, AI gives them the chance to grow and develop anytime, anyplace.

We know that you care about your child's schooling, and so do we. Because of this, AI is meant to help and support teachers, not replace them. AI tools help teachers plan lessons, make their own materials, and improve their skills. It's all about giving teachers the tools they need to make connections with students and adapt their lessons to each child's needs.

By using AI in education, you're giving your child a chance to do well in a digital world. AI literacy and understanding are important skills for the future, and putting AI into their education gives them the information and skills they need to deal with and take advantage of AI-driven advancements.

So, when you think about how important AI is for your child's education, keep in mind that AI is here to help them reach their full potential, customize their learning journey, and give them the tools they need to do well. Let's all take advantage of the power of AI and watch our kids soar in this exciting new era of education!

# THE TRANSFORMATIVE POWER OF AI IN PARENTING AND EDUCATION

**Imagine this:** AI in parenting and education is like having a super-smart helper by your side, ready to help your child succeed and make your job as a parent a little easier. It's really cool! Let me break down how AI can change things for you:

First of all, the goal is to learn in a way that fits your needs. AI programs dig deep into data about how your child learns, what they're good at, and where they might need more help. With this information, AI can make learning paths and materials that are tailored to your child's needs. It's like having a program made especially for them! This helps them understand the ideas better, stay engaged, and reach their full potential.

But that's not all! AI gives input and helpthose changes over time. Intelligent tutoring systems that are run by AI work like virtual tutors and give your child immediate feedback and help as they learn. If they get stuck on a hard idea, the AI tutor will help them get back on track by giving them helpful answers and links. It's like having a patient, knowledgeable tutor available 24 hours a day, 7 days a week.

Now, let's talk about events that are interactive and engage you in them. Virtual reality (VR) and augmented reality (AR), which are powered by AI, make learning a lot more fun and exciting. Imagine that your child could use VR to learn about other societies or do virtual science experiments. These hands-on activities pique their interest, make more fun, and help them understand difficult topics better.

AI also makes tasting and marking much easier. AI programs can look at what people have written and give grades in a flash. This means that teachers will have less time to spend on grading and more time to spend on giving personalized lessons and coaching. Also, AI can give your child specific feedback, which can help them learn from their mistakes and get better at what they do.

AI doesn't stop there, though! Its other purpose is to help you as a member. AI-powered smart baby monitors can keep an eye on your child's vital signs and sleep habits, giving you peace of mind and letting you know when they need help. Virtual companions are like having a trusted friend by your side. They offer evidence-based advice, methods for child development, and parenting tips that are based on the age and needs of your child. They are there to help you feel confident as you go through the ups and downs of dating.

With AI on your side, learning and schooling becomes more specialized, interesting, and useful. It's all about focusing on your child's unique skills, helping them grow, and making learning fun.

So, are you excited about how AI can change the way we teach and learn? In the next part, we'll go into more detail and look at specific ways that AI is changing the future of education. I got ready to be amazed by the amazing things that AI can do for teaching and learning. Let's continue our AI adventure together!

# HOW IS AI SHAPING THE FUTURE OF LEARNING?

AI is having a big impact on how people will learn in the future. There are some ways that AI is changing and affecting the way we teach and learn:

**Personalized Learning:**AI makes it possible for students to have learning experiences that are tailored to their needs, tastes, and learning styles. Intelligent tutoring systems can look at a student's performance data and give them feedback, advice, and suggestions that are specific to them. This helps them find their own ways to learn.

**Adaptive Assessment:** AI-based adaptive assessment uses machine learning algorithms to analyze students' answers in real time and change the level and type of questions based on how well they do. This makes it possible to test students' knowledge and skills more accurately and more quickly and to find their strengths and flaws.

**Data-Driven Decision Making:** AI makes it easier to collect and analyze data, which gives teachers and institutions important information about how students learn, how far they've come, and where they can improve. By using AI analytics, teachers can make choices based on data to improve their teaching methods, curriculum, and interventions.

**Intelligent Material Creation:** AI technologies can be used to make interactive textbooks, videos, and texts, as well as find and organize other educational materials. Natural Language Processing (NLP) makes it possible to create content automatically, which save teachers time and help them can make learning tools that are interesting and fun to use.

**Virtual Assistants and Chatbots:** Students can get help and support right away from virtual assistants and chatbots that are driven by AI. They can answer questions, explain things, and help students learn, giving them specific help and encouraging them to learn on their own.

**Language Learning and Translation:** AI technologies, such as speech recognition and machine translation, help people learn languages by giving them feedback in real time, letting them practice their vocabulary, and translating languages. This makes it easier for people to practice and converse in different languages.

**Accessibility and Inclusion:** AI can help make education easier for students with disabilities to get to and more accessible to them. For example, AI-based assistive tools can turn text into speech, provide closed captions, and give students who are deaf or hard of hearing other ways to communicate.

AI makes administrative jobs like grading, scheduling, and managing students easier. This lets teachers spend more time teaching and helping students, which improves performance overall.

**Lifelong Learning and Skill Development:** AI platforms can help with lifelong learning by giving personalized suggestions for up skilling and re-skilling based on each person's job goals and industry trends. AI can help people learn new skills and knowledge quickly so they can keep up with the changing needs of the job market.

**Collaboration and Social Learning:** AI can make it easier for students, teachers, and experts from different parts of the world to work together to learn. Virtual collaboration tools, online discussion platforms, and group work that is supported by AI can help students connect with each other and share what they know.

AI has many different effects on learning. It changes the way standard education works and gives students more control over their learning by giving them personalized, adaptable, and interesting experiences. It could help people get a better education, make it easier for them to learn, and give them the skills they need to do well in the future. But it's important to combine the use of AI with good teaching methods and ethical concerns to make sure that technology works as a supplement to how people teach and learn.

# OVERCOMING THE GENERATION GAP

We live in a time when technology and society are changing quickly, which is causing a gap between between parents and their children. But don't worry, because I have a glimpse of hope: Artificial intelligence, which can help close the gap and improve family ties.

AI's amazing skills have the potential to change the way we raise children and care for the next generation. It can be a beacon of light, a source of support and understanding, and a way for parents and children to talk to each other.

First of all, AI can help parents understand and meet their children's wants and goals. Its algorithms can look at data, patterns, and trends to tell us important things about their personalities, interests, and growth. With this information, parents can connect with their kid's better, appreciate their unique traits, and help their kids follow their passions.

AI can also help make sure that our children get a personalized schooling and learning experience. Its adaptive learning algorithms can figure out what each person is good at and what they need help with, so that educational material cans be made to fit their needs. This makes sure that every child gets a education that helps them reach their full potential. It also bridges the gap between old ways of teaching and the digital world, which is changing quickly.

But we shouldn't forget that AI has the power to improve emotional intelligence and mental health. Parenting can be hard, and AI can help parents who aren't sure what to do or are worried by giving them advice and support. AI-powered tools can give parents information, tips, and ways to deal with the challenges of raising children. This gives them the knowledge they need to be good caregivers.

AI can also help families get along well by making it easier for people to talk to each other and share experiences. Intelligent virtual assistants can be used as mediators to help families work out their problems and have productive talks. By using AI, parents can create an environment of confidence, empathy, and mutual understanding with their children. This strengthens the bond between parents and children and closes the gap between generations.

Friends, there is a lot that AI could do to help people from different generations work together. It gives us a chance to make our homes a place where the wisdom of old age and the energy of youth can live together and grow. Let's welcome this technology and remember that it can help us be better partners, not replace us.

Remember that the goal of every bit of code, every algorithm, and every AI-powered tool is to make life better for people. It is up to us to use its power to help our families and the people who will come after us.

So, parents, let's use AI as a friend, a partner, and a source of ideas on this amazing journey of parenting. Let's work together to close the gap between generations, build stronger ties, and raise a generation that is strong, kind, and ready to make the world a better place.

# SECTION 3

# ENSURING SAFETY AND WELL BE-ING

# SAFEGUARDING CHILDREN IN THE DIGITAL AGE:

How AI makes monitoring better and makes sure people are safe online and offline.

AI can be a very important part of keeping children safe, both online and offline. AI can help in the following ways:

**Content Filtering:**

AI-powered systems can analyze and filter internet content, making it harder for kids to get exposed to things that aren't good for them or are harmful. AI can find and block materials that may be harmful or inappropriate for children by using natural language processing and image recognition. This makes the Internet a safer place for kids to be online.

**Parental Controls:**

AI-based parental control tools let parents set rules and limits for their children's individual actions that are specific to each child. These tools can help parents control how much time their kid spends in front of a screen, block certain websites or apps, and get advice or reports on their child's only behavior to keep them safe.

**How to Find Cyber bullying:**

AI programs can look at how people talk to each other online and spot signs of abuse or harassment. By keeping an eye on social media, chat apps, and other online channels, AI can warn parents or guardians about possible dangers and help them protect their child's safety.

## Tracking the Location:

Geolocation data can be used by AI-powered tracking tools to help parents know where their child is at all times. This can be especially helpful for making sure kids are safe when they are away from home or in places they don't know.

## Detection of Threats:

AI can look at online chats, emails, and texts to find possible threats or cases of "grooming." AI can spot dangerous behavior by using natural language processing and machine learning. This lets parents take the right steps to protect their child from possible harm.

## Facial Recognition:

Face recognition technology that is driven by AI can be used to keep an eye on who interacts with your child both online and offline. This can add a layer of security by letting you know who is allowed in and spotting any suspicious faces that could be dangerous.

## Response to an Emergency:

AI systems can be connected to energy response systems to help people quickly when they need it. AI-powered devices, for example, can instantly look for signs of distress, call for help, or tell certain people if a child is in danger or needs help right away.

By using AI technologies to keep an eye on children and make sure they are safe, parents can rest easy knowing that their kids are safe both online and in the real world.

# CHALLENGES IN AI:
# CHALLENGES OF AI IN KIDS' EDUCATION

There are many ways that artificial intelligence (AI) can help kids learn, but there are also some problems that need to be fixed. Here are the most important problems with using AI to teach kids:

**Data Privacy and Security:** For AI to work, a lot of data, including personal information, needs to be collected and analyzed. It is very important to protect the privacy and protection of children's data because it contains sensitive information. Safeguards and processes must be in place to prevent data from being used or accessed by people who shouldn't be able to.

**Bias and Fairness:** AI systems can correct biases that are already present in the data they use to train themselves. This can lead to unfair results or make differences worse. It is important to fix bias in AI algorithms, especially in educational software, so that all students have fair and equal chances.

**Lack of Human Interaction:** AI-based learning tools and systems can make learning more personalized, but they may not have the human touch. Social-emotional learning and human interaction are important parts of schooling. In the learning process, it's important to find a good balance between AI-driven personalization and keeping useful human connections.

**Ethical Considerations and Transparency:** AI programs can be hard to understand because they can be complicated and hard to see how they make decisions or suggestions. It is important that AI systems used in education are open and clear, so that students, parents, and teachers can understand how they work and trust that they are the best.

**Overuse of AI:** AI can help people learn, but using too many AI-based tools and platforms can make it harder to think critically, solve problems, and be creative. AI should be used as a supplement to human teaching, not as an alternative to it. This will encourage students to take an active role in the learning process.

**Access That Is Fair:** People from different communities and socio-economic backgrounds may not have the same amount of access to AI tools and digital resources. It is important to close the digital divide and give all students, regardless of their socio-economic status, equal access to AI tools and educational possibilities.

**Development of Ethical AI Skills:** As AI becomes more common, it is important to teach children about the ethical factors and effects of AI. They need to know how to use AI in a responsible way, how it affects privacy, how bias works, and what might happen if they only used information made by AI.

**Training and Help for Teachers:** Adding AI to the classroom requires teachers to get the right training and help. Teachers need to know how to use AI tools and platforms in their lessons, how to understand the data generated by AI, and how to help students with advice and support using AI-driven educational resources.

**Continuous Monitoring and Evaluation:** Algorithms and systems that use AI need to be constantly monitored and evaluated to make sure they are working, relevant, and in line with educational goals. Regular evaluations and ways to get feedback are needed to find any problems or areas that need to be fixed.

By tackling these problems ahead of time, people who care about kids' education can use AI's potential while minimizing risks and making sure it is used in a responsible and inclusive way in the learning process.

# PRACTICAL STEPS FOR ENSURING FAMILY'S DIGITAL SAFETY

Practical Steps for Ensuring Families Digital Safety and Privacy in an AI-Driven World

In a world run by AI, it's very important to make sure your family's internet security and privacy are protected. Here are some easy things you can do to protect your family's privacy and keep them safe online:

**You And Your Family Should Learn:**

- Stay up to date on the latest issues and risks related to privacy and AI technologies.
- Inform yourself and your family about privacy settings, how to stay safe online, and what might happen if you share personal information online.

**Passwords That Are Strong and Unique:**

- Encourage your family to use strong, unique passwords for their Internet accounts.
- Use a password organizer to store and make passwords in a safe way.

**Connecting To the Internet Safely:**

- Use Wi-Fi services that are safe and encrypted at home.
- Change the usual login information and keep the router's firmware up to date.

- Keep your devices and software up to date.

- Make sure that your family's working systems, apps, and devices are always up to date.

- Make sure you have the latest security fixes and features by turning on automatic updates.

**Meetings for Privacy and Permissions:**

- Review the privacy settings on the devices, apps, and internet services that your family uses and make any necessary changes.

- Limit the amount of information you share and take away rights from apps that want too much access to your personal information.

- Limit the sharing of personal information.

- Tell your family, especially your kids, to be careful about what personal information they share online.

- Teach them to only give out information that is needed on sites that are trusted and safe.

**Pay Attention to Social Medicine:**

- Teach your family members how important it is to keep their social media choices private.

- Tell them to be careful about what they share with the world and to limit who can see their personal information.

**Use Software And Tools For Safety:**

Malicious threats can be stopped by installing antivirus and anti-malware software from a reputable company.

Think about using a virtual private network (VPN) to protect your online activities and encrypt your internet data.

**Watch What People Do Online:**

- Watch what your family does online, especially if your kids are young.
- Encourage open discussion and set rules for using the Internet in a responsible way.
- Review and delete data often.
- Review your devices, apps, and web accounts often and delete any personal information that is no longer needed.
- Be aware of the data that AI-driven systems collect, and if you can, consider not letting them collect data.

**Adhere To The Policies On Privacy:**

- Read the privacy policies of the apps and internet services that your family uses and make sure you understand them.
- Look for platforms that put user privacy and the security of their information first.

**Help People Think Critically:**

- Teach your family to think carefully about what they read and to question the accuracy and reliability of material made by AI. Help them learn to be skeptical and to get information from more than one source.

Don't forget that privacy and digital security require constant care and attention. In an AI-driven world, you can help protect your family's digital privacy and keep the internet a safer place by taking these steps.

59

# WAYS TO MENTAL HEALTH AND WELL BEING

AI has the ability to help kids in many ways with their mental health and well-being. AI can help with checking and assessing maternal health, which is one area where it can be useful. By studying written or spoken text with Natural Language Processing (NLP) algorithms, AI-powered tools can help find possible signs of distress. This allows for early intervention and helps get a true picture of a child's maternal health.

Personalized solutions are another way AI can help kids be healthy and happy. Virtual assistants or chatbots with AI algorithms can help in a way that is engaging and personalized. Depending on the needs and preferences of each child, it can give coping techniques, mindful exercises, or suggestions for good resources. This personalized method can make it easier for kids to get involved and help their mental health.

Face recognition and sensory analysis are examples of AI technologies that can recognize and understand feelings. This opens the door for AI-powered tools that can help and give feedback to children in real time. By figuring out how children are feeling, these tools can give them the right answers or suggestions, which helps them handle their feelings well.

Applications that use virtual reality (VR) or augmented reality (AR) and are powered by AI can build immersive and interactive therapies.

Through exposure therapy or other relaxation methods, these experiences can help children deal with stress, anxiety, or phobias. AI-enabled therapeutic support can help improve the efficiency of interventions and the health and well-being of children by creating a safe and controlled environment.

Wearable devices or mobile apps that are driven by AI can track physical signs of emotional health like heart rate, sleep patterns, or stress levels. This information can help us understand how a child is feeling and find possible triggers or trends. By knowing these things, parents and professionals can help a child's mental health and well-being in the best way possible.

AI can also personalize educational materials and resources to help kids learn about and take care of their mental health and well-being. Based on a child's interests and needs, AI algorithms can find articles, videos, or interactive materials that are important to them. This personalized method can help with education and teach kids how to help themselves, giving them the tools, they need to keep their mental health in decent shape.

AI systems can look at children's patterns of behavior and early warning signs to see if they are at risk for maternal health problems. AI can let guardians or teachers know about possible problems by noticing patterns of behavior or changes in how a person talks. This lets them help the person right away. This early discovery can make a significant difference in helping children have better maternal health.

AI tools can also make it easier for children with disabilities to get help with their mental health. Text-to-speech, visual tools, or adaptive activities can make it easier for children with hearing, visual, or cognitive impairments to use mental health resources. AI-based solutions can close the enterprise gap and make sure that all kids have the same chances to get maternal health help.

AI can be helpful, but it shouldn't take the place of people. Instead, it should work alongside them. Children need help from people, like mental health workers, caregivers, and teachers, to make sure they are healthy and get the emotional support and guidance they need. AI-powered tools and human knowledge can be used together to help children's mental health and well-being in a comprehensive and all-around way.

# STRATEGIES FOR MAINTAINING A HEALTHY BALANCE WITH TECHNOLOGY.

In today's digital age, it's important to keep a good balance with technology. There are some things you can do to find and keep that balance:

One way to deal with technology in the family is to set clear limits and rules. Set aside times and places without screens, like during meals or before bed, to support face-to-face time and quality time together. Make places in your house like the bedroom where technology isn't allowed to help you sleep and reduce distractions.

Another important thing to do is show kids how to use technology in a healthy way. Children often act the same way as the people they see. Parents can have a good effect on their children's behavior by showing them how to use technology in a healthy way, such as by not spending too much time in front of a screen, doing things off-line, and putting real-world connections first.

It's important to talk to kids in an open and continuing way. Talk about the pros and cons of technology and encourage people to talk about how to use it safely. Teach kids how important it is to be aware of themselves and how to control themselves when using technology. Tell them to think about how technology affects their health and happiness and to look into other activities and hobbies.

Adding hobbies and routines that don't involve technology can help restore balance. Encourage kids to play outside, do artistic things, or have hobbies that don't involve screaming. Encourage reading, playing outside, arts and crafts, and other things that bring people together and take them away from their screens.

Use the built-in tools on devices and apps to improve your digital health. Use parental controls and app limits to control how much time your child spends on the screen and what they can see. Use tools that remind you or limit notifications to help you stay focused and not be interrupted.

Promote a healthy digital diet by highlighting good materials and learning tools. Help kids learn how to think critically and understand how to use multimedia so they can find their way around the huge digital world. Encourage them to read and watch things that are helpful, upbeat, and in line with their interests and beliefs.

Evaluate and reevaluate how your family uses technology often. Check how technology affects your general well-being and make changes as needed. Encourage children to think about themselves and control themselves. This will give them the opportunity to make informed decisions about how they use technology and find their own balance.

Lastly, use technology in a way that is adaptable and efficient. Technology is a big part of life today, and its role keeps changing. Accept the good things about technology while keeping a healthy perspective and knowing when to make changes or set limits.

# SECTION 4

# ETHICAL CONSIDERATIONS AND FUTURE PERSPECTIVES.

# ETHICS WHEN USING TECHNOLOGY

It's important to think about ethics when using technology, including AI, to make sure that things turn out well. There are some important things to keep in mind.

**Privacy and Data Protection:** Be careful with people's personal information and respect their right to privacy. Ask for permission to gather information and be clear about how it will be used. Keep data safe so that no one can get to it or use it without permission.

**Transparency and Ability to Be Explained:** Make sure that AI systems are clear and easy to understand. They should be able to explain why they did what they did and how they did it. Inform users of any risks, limits, or biases that come with AI technologies. Don't use formulas that are too hard to figure out.

**Bias and Fairness:** Watch out for biases in data and programs that could lead to unfair results. Check AI systems for flaws often and take steps to fix them if you find them. Make sure AI systems are trained on a wide range of data so they don't reinforce biases that are already there.

**Accountability and Responsibility:** Make it clear who is in charge of making AI systems and keeping an eye on them. Set up ways to deal with any harm that AI technologies might cause. Think about what AI means for society, business, and the environment as a whole.

**Human-Centric Sign:** When making and using AI systems, put the well-being, safety, and respect of people first. Think about how AI might change how people make decisions, act on their own, and connect with each other. Include morals and ethics in the process of growth.

**Informed Consent and User Empowerment:** Give users control over their data and the ability to make well-informed decisions. Explain what using AI systems means and what could go wrong. Let the people who use AI decide how they want to connect with it.

**Impact on Society and the Environment:** Think about AI's larger impact on society, such as on jobs, inequality, and the environment. Use AI to help solve problems in society and bring about good change. Try to get AI to help with social growth and long-term sustainability.

**Continuous Monitoring and Evaluation:** Keep track of and evaluate AI systems over time to figure out how they affect ethics. Listen to what people say and make changes as needed. Encourage independent audits to make sure that people are acting ethically.

**Collaboration and Engagement:** To solve ethical problems, work with researchers, policymakers, businesses, and civil society. Discuss the ethics of AI from different points of view. Get people involved in making ethical rules for AI.

We can use AI in a responsible and ethical way if we think about these ethical issues. This makes sure that AI systems look out for our best interests, respect our values, and help society.

# IMPORTANCE OF CRITICAL THINKING

We will talk about how critical thinking is important and how AI can help develop this important skill:

In today's complicated and quickly changing world, it is important to be able to think critically. It lets people look at information, judge its reliability and usefulness, and make decisions based on that knowledge. AI can help and improve critical thinking skills in a number of ways.

AI can help by giving people access to a huge amount of knowledge. Search engines and databases that are powered by AI can quickly get information from many different sources, letting people get different points of view and proof. People can find it hard to sort through all of this information and figure out which sources are reliable and which ones aren't.

AI can also help people evaluate information by giving them tools to check facts and sources. Automated fact-checking algorithms can look at claims and match them to information from reliable sources. This helps people spot content that is false or misleading. This gives people who can think critically the tools they need to question and check information before they accept it as true.

AI technologies can also show different views and points of view. Recommendation systems and personalized content algorithms can show people different points of view, which can challenge their ideas and make them think about other points of view. This helps people become more open-minded, intellectually flexible, and able to examine and combine different points of view.

AI can also help people think critically by giving them tools for analyzing and displaying data. AI programs can analyze and make sense of large amounts of data to find patterns, trends, and insights. AI-powered visualizations and data analysis tools can help people study and understand data better, so they can come to correct conclusions and make decisions based on facts.

Also, AI-powered virtual helpers or chatbots can start conversations and give people chances to practice critical thinking. By asking people probing questions, showing them hypothetical situations, and challenging their ideas, these AI-powered tools can help people think more deeply and figure out how to solve complex problems.

But it's important to remember that even though AI can help people think critically, it shouldn't replace human thought or take the place of independent analysis and judgment. Critical thought requires creativity, intuition, and thinking about what right and wrong, which AI may not be able to do fully.

In today's information-driven world, it's important to be able to think critically, and AI can help people develop this skill. AI technologies can help people develop and improve their critical thinking skills by giving them access to information, helping them evaluate information, showing them different points of view, helping them analyze data, and having conversations with them. By accepting the synergy between human thought and AI, people can become better critical thinkers who can deal with complicated problems and make better decisions.

# STRATEGIC STEPS TO KEEP PRIVACY AND MAKE GOOD DECISIONS

In an AI-driven world, it takes careful attention and strategic steps to keep privacy and make good decisions. Here are some ways to make this happen:

**Learn about Data Privacy Policies:** Learn about the privacy policies of the AI systems and sites you use. Learn how your information is gathered, used, and shared. Look for platforms that put user privacy and the safety of their info first.

**Control Data Sharing:** Becareful about the personal information you share online and with AI systems. Only give the information that is needed and thinks about the possible risks of giving sensitive information. Review and change the privacy settings on your devices, apps, and online services on a regular basis to stop sharing data that isn't necessary.

**Educate Yourself:** Stay up to data on the latest privacy issues and risks that come with AI technologies. Know what it means to collect data and how it might affect your privacy. Learn   the best ways to keep your personal information safe in an AI-driven world.

**Choose Tools That Protect Your Privacy:** Use tools and systems that protect your privacy. Use   virtual private networks (VPNs), for instance, to encrypt internet data and keep online activities save. Think about using browsers and search engines that put privacy and security first.

**Responsible Data Management:** Do what you can to handle your data in a responsible way. Review your devices, apps, and web accounts often and delete any personal information that is no longer needed. Be aware of the data that AI systems collect, and if you can, try to stop them from doing so.

When you use AI systems or platforms, make sure you read and understand the terms of service and user agreements. Be sure you know what data rights you are giving away and how your data could be used. Be careful about agreeing to rules that require you to give out personal information.

**Demand Transparency:** Try to get AI systems to be open. Encourage companies and coders to share the information they gather, the algorithms they use, and how they make decisions. Help projects that support openness and the right way to use AI.

**Use AI In A Ethical Way:** Think about the ethical aspects of the technologies you use and the possible results of your choices. When making decisions, think about how fair AI systems are, if they are biased, and how they affect society. Try to use AI in a way that fits with your goals and encourages you to make good decisions.

**Find Sources You Can Trust:** When depending on information or suggestions made by AI, think carefully about how credible and reliable the sources are. Check information from more than one source and check facts when you need to. Be wary of AI-generated material that may contain false information or a bias.

**Stay In The Process Of Making Decisions:** Take part in making AI systems and putting them into place. Protect people's privacy and act in a reasonable way. Take part in conversations, give feedback, and help shape the rules and policies that guide AI technology.

By using these tactics, people can live in an AI-driven world while still keeping their privacy and making good decisions. It takes being proactive, learning new things all the time, and being aware of the possible risks and ethical issues that come with AI technologies.

# LEARN ABOUT CAREERS IN AI AND GET READY FOR SUCCESS:

There are a lot of different and interesting jobs in the field of AI, and helping kid's succeed in this fast-changing field can be an exciting task. Here are some steps kids can take to learn about careers in AI and get ready for success:

**Encourage Interest and Curiosity:** Get kids interested in and curious about AI-related ideas and tools. Show them how AI is used in everyday life and talk with them about its effects and possibilities. Encourage a love of learning and fixing problems, which are important skills for AI.

**Build a Strong Foundation:** Give math, statistics, and computer science a lot of attention. These are the most important parts of AI. Encourage kids to do well in these areas and to take classes or do things outside of school that will help them learn more about algorithms, programming, and data analysis.

**Engage in AI-related Projects and Competitions:** Encourage people to take part in AI-related projects, competitions, or hackathons. Children can use their skills, work with their friends, and learn more about AI development, machine learning, or robotics through these hands-on activities. This helps them get better at fixing problems and working as a team.

**Encourage Critical Thinking and Creativity:** Teach children how to think critically by asking them to examine problems, find patterns, and come up with new ways to solve them. Encourage them to think outside of the box and come up with new ideas. AI works best when people think creatively, so it's important to work on this skill if you want to do well in the field.

**Find Guidance And Mentorship:** Put kids in touch with adults who work in areas related to AI. Mentors can help with job advice, guidance, and new ideas. They can talk about their own experiences, suggest ways to learn, and show how AI is used in the real world. Mentoring helps people grow as people and helps kids make smart choices about their careers.

**Pursue Education that's Useful:** Help your kids go to college in areas like computer science, data science, or AI-specific programs. Tell them to look for universities or other places that are known for their study and programs in AI. Internships and joint education programs can give you real-world experience and connections in the field.

**Focus on Cross-Disciplinary Skills:** Talk about how important cross-disciplinary skills are for AI jobs. Encourage kids to learn about other things, like psychology, ethics, or business, because they can help shape how AI is used. In the area of AI, it's helpful to have good communication, teamwork, and moral reasoning skills.

**Stay Current and Adapt:** Encourage people to keep learning and keep up with the latest AI developments. The field changes quickly, so kids should be ready to learn new tools, methods, and industry trends. Encourage them to go to conferences, workshops, or online groups to stay in touch with people who work in AI.

**Encourage Ethical AI Use:** Stress how important it is to think about ethics and use AI in a responsible way. Instill in children the values of kindness, openness, and responsibility in their work with AI. Encourage them to think about how AI apps will affect society and how they will affect ethics, and to do something good for the field.

**Encourage Collaboration and Networking:** Give kids chances to work together and meet new people by getting them to talk to their peers, join AI-related teams or groups, and go to AI-related events. Collaboration and networking give them a chance to see things from different points of view and grow their business networks.

By doing these things, you can help kids get ahead in the field of AI. With a solid foundation, a desire to learn, critical thinking skills, and a ethical mindset, they can navigate the exciting and always-changing world of AI and make important contributions to its growth and use.

# NURTURING DIGITAL INTELLIGENCE

How apps that use artificial intelligence help busy parents manage their time and give their kids the best care possible

How artificial intelligence can help young people be more creative and interested.

**Online Growth of Artificial Intelligence:**

Using artificial intelligence to help your child grows and learn.

There are many good things that can happen when AI technology is used in a child's growth, but it needs to be done carefully and in a responsible way. Here are some things to think about and ideas to try as you think about how to raise your child with AI:

**AI Software for Schools:**

Look into AI-powered learning systems, apps, and tools that are good for kids. Your child can get instruction and feedback based on his or her own interests and skills with these tools.

**How to Get Better at Critical Thinking Online:**

Talk to your child about what artificial intelligence can do and what it can't. Give students the tools they need to think critically about the material made by AI, spot any biases, and understand the ethical issues that come up when using it.

Use artificial intelligence to make it easier for people to work in groups and learn together. Your child may learn how to work in a team, solve problems, and think creatively, and they may also learn how AI and humans can work well together.

**AI and Creative Expression:** Show your child some AI tools that can help them be more creative in how they express themselves. They can be pushed to be creative by giving them AI-enhanced platforms for music composition, visual arts, or storytelling.

Moral AI Talk about your worries about privacy, data security, and fairness as they relate to the use of AI. Teach your child how to be a good digital citizen by teaching them how important it is to protect the privacy of others and how to recognize and avoid bias in AI.

**AI in Everyday Life:** People use things like smart gadgets, voice assistants, and recommendation systems every day that use AI. Show me how AI works and give me some ways it could make my life easier or more productive.

**Make People Curious and Wonder:**Help your child learn more about artificial intelligence. Get kids are involved in talks, projects, and activities about AI that are right for their ages.

AI can be helpful, but it's important to find a good mix between it and human interaction. Make sure your child has a lot of one-on-one conversations, group activities, and off-screen situations to help them develop their social and emotional skills.

**Emphasize How To Make AI That Helps Everyone:**Help your child thinks about AI as a possible subject or future job. Get them to help make AI systems that are fair for everyone and good for society as a whole.

Keep up with what's going on in the field of artificial intelligence (AI) in terms of new ideas, research, and ethical discussions. After reading this, you'll be better able to help your child make good choices about how to use AI in a responsible way.

Your family's views, the child's age, and the child as a whole should guide how you use artificial intelligence (AI) to help raise your child. If you teach kids about AI and how to use it in a moral way, you can give them the skills they need to do well in a world where AI is the norm.

# HOW AI EMPOWERS COGNITIVE DEVELOPMENT AND PROBLEM-SOLVING SKILLS IN CHILDREN.

AI-powered gadgets and apps can help a child learn to think and solve problems in a big way. Here are some of the ways they can help.

**Personalized Learning:** AI can change to fit a child's learning style and pace, making learning experiences unique to each child. By looking at a child's strengths, weaknesses, and growth, AI can give them personalized content and challenges that help them learn to think and solve problems.

**Adaptive Tutoring:**Tutoring systems that are powered by AI can give kid's feedback and help as they work through hard tasks. These systems can figure out where a kid might be having trouble and help them in those areas, which helps them learn to think critically and solve problems.

**Gamified Learning:** AI can use game-like methods to make learning more fun and interactive. AI-powered applications can encourage children to think freely, plan ahead, and solve problems in a fun way by adding game elements like rewards, challenges, and interactive simulations.

**Intelligent Assistants:** Virtual assistants that are driven by AI can act as friends for children by answering their questions, having talks with them, and stimulating their minds. These helpers can help kids learn to think critically, ask questions that make them think, and try out new ideas. This improves their cognitive skill.

**Analysis of Data:** AI can look at a lot of educational data and find patterns or trends in how a child learns. This information can be used to find areas where a child needs to improve, offer good learning resources, and make sure that a child's educational experiences meet his or her unique cognitive needs.

**Collaborative Problem Solving:** AI-powered apps can make it easier for kids to work together to solve hard problems. AI can improve both cognitive and social skills at the same time by encouraging teamwork, communication, and making decisions as a group.

**Simulation and Modeling:** Tools that use AI to run simulations and models can create virtual worlds where kids can play, learn, and experiment. Through hands-on experiences, these tools can help children learn how to solve problems, figure out what causes what, and get a better grasp on complicated ideas.

By using AI-powered devices and apps, parents can give their kids an invaluable chance of improving their cognitive skills, solving problems ability, and developing the love of learning that will last a lifetime.

# THE BENEFITS OF AI-POWERED PERSONALIZED LEARNING FOR CHILDREN'S INDIVIDUAL NEEDS AND INTERESTS

Using AI to make learning experiences that are tailored to a child's needs and hobbies can have a number of possible benefits. Some of them are:

**Individualized Instruction:** AI can change educational content and materials based on a child's unique skills, weaknesses, and learning style. AI can improve engagement and understanding by making the learning experience fit each person's needs. This leads to better learning results.

**Improved Engagement and Motivation:** Learning experiences that are tailored to a child's hobbies can make them more interested, more motivated, and more engaged. AI can suggest interesting topics, activities, and multimedia tools that will keep a child's attention and make learning more fun.

**Flexible Pace and Progression:** Platforms that are powered by AI can let kids learn at their own pace, giving them extra help or tasks as they need it. Adaptive algorithms can track a child's progress and change the level of difficulty or the material based on that. This makes sure that the child learns the most without getting too frustrated or bored.

**Targeted Remediation:** AI can figure out where a child may be having trouble and offer targeted interventions or tools to help them. AI can help kids work through problems and understand tough ideas better by giving them personalized feedback, adaptive exercises, and more practice materials.

**Expanding Horizons:** AI-powered systems can teach kids about a wider range of themes and topics than what is usually taught in school. By looking at a child's hobbies and how they've learned in the past, AI can suggest related areas of study. This helps them learn new things and encourages them to explore.

**Continuous Assessment and Feedback:** AI can test and give feedback on a child's learning all the time to keep track of how well the child is learning. AI can give children quick feedback, track their progress, and help them reach their learning goals by looking at their performance data and figuring out where they can improve.

**Lifelong Learning Skills:** AI-driven personalized learning experiences can teach children important 21st-century skills like critical thought, problem-solving, and self-directed learning. AI can help children become permanent learners who can handle the challenges of the future by encouraging them to think for themselves and be flexible.

Parents and teachers can help kid's reach their full potential, develop a love of learning, and get the skills they need to succeed in a world that is changing quickly by using AI to create personalized learning experiences.

# EFFICIENCY AND CARE:

How do AI-powered tools help busy parents balance their responsibilities and give their kids the care they need?

AI-powered tools can help parents with their busy plans take good care of their kids while still getting everything else done. Here are a few ways that AI can help:

**Intelligent Scheduling:** AI can help parents manage their time more effectively by looking at their schedules, goals, and responsibilities. AI-powered calendars can suggest the best times for activities, help plan family events, and remind parents to stay on track.

**Smart Home Automation:** AI can automate everyday jobs in the home, like adjusting the lighting, temperature, or playing soothing music. This makes the home a safe and comfortable place for children to grow up in. This system can save parents time and energy so they can spend more time with their kids.

AI-powered virtual assistants can be used as personal organizers to do things like set reminders, make to-do lists, and keep track of meetings. Parents can count on these assistants to help them stay organized, which gives them more mental space to be more focused and attentive parents.

**Child Safety and Monitoring:** AI-powered monitoring systems can give parents real-time reports on what their child is doing, making sure they are safe even when they are busy with other things. AI can tell parents, for example, when a child leaves a certain place or if any possible safety risks are found.

**Educational Support:** Educational apps and platforms that are built on AI can help a child learn and grow. Even when they can't be there in person, parents can use these tools to give their kids educational material, interactive exercises, and virtual tutoring sessions.

AI-powered conversation tools can make it easier for parents and children to talk to each other from far away. Even when they can't be with their kids in person, parents can stay in touch and have important conversations with them through video calls, messaging apps, and even virtual reality.

**Analysis of Data and Insights:**

AI can look at data about children's habits, behavior patterns, and preferences to help parents make better choices. For example, AI can suggest things that are good for a child's age, suggest healthy sleep schedules, or give nutritional advice. This helps parents take the best care of their children.

Parents can handle their busy lives and take good care of their kids at the same time by using tools that are powered by AI. These technologies can make chores easier, give support, and give parents peace of mind, so they can juggle their responsibilities while still being there for their kids and caring about their well-being.

# NURTURING IMAGINATION:

How does AI make kids more creative and encourage them to explore?

AI can help children develop their curiosity and imagination in a number of ways. AI can help and encourage creative thinking in the following ways:

**Generative Art and Music:** Algorithms that are driven by artificial intelligence can make original art or music. These can give children ideas and show them new ways to be creative. AI-made art and music can be explored by children, which can spark their own creative ideas and encourage artistic expression.

**Help with Storytelling and Writing:** AI can help children with storytelling and writing by giving them ideas, prompts, and help with grammar or words. AI-powered writing tools can help kids improve their creativity and story-telling skills, so they can write their own imaginative stories.

**Virtual Reality and Simulation:** Virtual reality and simulations that are driven by artificial intelligence can take kids to imaginative and interactive worlds. These immersive settings can encourage kids to explore, solve problems, and play with their imaginations. They can also foster creativity by giving kids a place to try out new things and make things.

**Creative Coding and Programming:** AI can teach kids how to code and program by giving them tools and platforms that are fun to use. By doing coding projects, kids can learn computational thinking, problem-solving skills, and creativity as they create and build their own interactive apps or games.

**AI-driven Toys and Games:** Toys and games that are driven by AI can give kids the chance to be creative and interact with each other. From virtual reality building blocks to interactive storytellers, these AI-powered toys and games can help kids use their imaginations, solve problems, and think creatively.

**Collaborative AI Projects:** AI can help kids work on creative projects together, either with AI-powered virtual friends or with peers in different places. By working together on projects that use AI to make art, music, or stories, kids can learn from each other, share ideas, and discover new creative realms as a group.

**Creative Data Exploration:** AI can look at big sets of data and show ideas in ways that are pleasing to the eye. Children can interact with AI-made visualizations, patterns, and connections, which can help them think freely and look at science, technology, and art from new angles.

By using AI in creative projects, children can be introduced to new tools, ideas, and experiences that help them develop their imagination, learn to think critically, and build on their natural creative skills.

# INSIGHTS FOR EARLY INTERVENTION:

How AI helps track and analyze child health and development milestones for early intervention?

**Introduction:**

Monitoring and evaluating a child's health and growth is an important part of being a parent and teaching young children. With the development of artificial intelligence (AI), there are now new ways to use technology in this very important area. This chapter looks at how AI can help track and analyze children's health and development milestones, which can give useful information and improve their overall health.

**Growth Tracking Can Be Done Automatically:** Tools with AI can automatically keep track of a child's growth by analyzing data like height, weight, and head size. With the help of advanced algorithms and machine learning, these tools can find deviations from expected growth patterns and alert parents and medical experts to possible problems so they can act quickly.

**Behavior Analysis and Developmental Delays:** AI algorithms can look at speech, social relations, and motor skills, among other things, to find signs of possible developmental delays. By comparing a child's actions to known stages, AI systems can let parents and teachers know about areas that may need more attention or specific help.

**Early Detection of Developmental Disorders:** Artificial intelligence (AI) technology can help find developmental disorders like autism spectrum disorder (ASD) early on. AI algorithms can find subtle signs of ASD by looking at speech patterns, facial expressions, and how people connect with each other. Early detection allows for early assistance, which helps both the child and their family.

**Predictive Analytics for Developmental Trajectories:** AI can look at large amounts of data about a child's health and development to find patterns and make predictions about how the child will grow in the future. By knowing what causes good or bad outcomes, parents and health care workers can step in early and give a child the help he or she needs to grow and develop in the best way possible.

**Recommendations and Interventions Tailored to You:**

Based on each child's profile, AI-powered systems can give unique suggestions and interventions. AI can support a child's unique needs by taking into account things like genetic predispositions, environmental influences, and past health records. These things include nutrition, physical exercise, and educational interventions.

When AI is used to track a child's health and growth, it opens up new opportunities for early detection, tailored interventions, and better results. By using the power of AI algorithms, parents and medical workers can get useful information, improve early care, and make sure that children get the best care possible. As we look into the possibilities of AI in this area, we must also think about ethics and put people first. We can use AI as a tool to help us learn more and support children's health and growth. Let's all take advantage of AI's potential to change the way we track and analyze a child's health and growth for a better future.

**Unlocking Possibilities:**

A Practical Guide for Parents to Introduce AI and Work with It

**Engaging Pathways:**

Introducing Children to AI Concepts and Benefits in a Fun and Age-Appropriate Way

**Safeguarding Our Digital Journey:**

Practical Steps for Ensuring Family's Digital Safety and Privacy in an AI-Driven World

**Nurturing Ethical Minds:**

How Parents Can Foster Critical Thinking and Ethical Considerations in Children Regarding AI Technology

**Pathways to the Future:**

Exploring Career Opportunities in AI and Guiding Children towards Success

Ethical Considerations and Responsible AI Usage

**Guiding Principles:** Discuss the importance of teaching children about the ethical use of AI and technology. Explore topics such as data privacy, AI biases, and responsible AI development to ensure children develop a critical and ethical approach towards technology.

**Parental Guidance and Supervision:** Emphasize the role of parents in providing guidance and supervision to ensure responsible AI usage. Discuss strategies for setting boundaries, promoting healthy technology habits, and fostering open discussions about AI's impact on society.

In this chapter, we have explored the imperative of AI knowledge in modern parenting. By embracing AI, parents can bridge the generation gap, enhance communication, and foster empathy and adaptability in their children. However, it is essential to approach AI with caution, emphasizing ethical considerations and responsible usage. By embracing AI knowledge, you can become a guiding force in your children's lives, empowering them to navigate the digital landscape with confidence and shaping a future where technology and humanity coexist harmoniously.

**Insights for Early Intervention:**

How AI Supports Tracking and Analyzing Child Health and Development Milestones.

AI can be a valuable tool for tracking and analyzing a child's health and development milestones, offering valuable insights that can aid in early intervention if necessary. Here is some ways AI can assist in this regard:

**Growth Monitoring:**

AI-powered systems can analyze data such as height, weight, and body mass index (BMI) to track a child's growth over time. By comparing this data to standard growth charts, AI can identify potential growth patterns or deviations, alerting parents or healthcare professionals to potential concerns.

**Developmental Milestone Tracking:**

AI can help track a child's developmental milestones, such as motor skills, language development, and cognitive abilities. By analyzing data collected through observation or interaction with AI-powered tools, parents and healthcare providers can gain insights into a child's progress and identify any potential developmental delays.

**Speech and Language Assessment:**

AI can assist in assessing a child's speech and language development by analyzing recordings or interactions. Using natural language processing and machine learning techniques, AI can evaluate language skills, identify potential speech disorders, and recommend appropriate interventions or therapies.

**Behavioral Pattern Analysis:**

AI algorithms can analyze behavioral patterns and detect potential indicators of developmental issues or emotional well-being. By processing data collected from wearable devices, smart home sensors, or other sources, AI can identify patterns that may require further evaluation or intervention.

**Early Detection of Health Conditions:**

AI can assist in the early detection of health conditions or risk factors by analyzing various types of data, such as genetic information, medical records, or environmental factors. By identifying potential red flags or correlations, AI can provide valuable insights that facilitate early intervention and treatment.

**Predictive Analytics:**

AI can leverage historical data and predictive analytics to forecast potential health issues or developmental risks. By analyzing patterns and trends, AI can generate risk assessments, allowing parents and healthcare providers to take proactive measures for prevention or early intervention.

**Personalized Health Recommendations:**

AI-powered systems can provide personalized health recommendations based on a child's health data and specific needs. These recommendations can include suggestions for nutrition, exercise, sleep, and overall well-being, promoting healthy habits and supporting optimal development.

By leveraging AI for tracking and analyzing a child's health and development milestones, parents and healthcare professionals can gain valuable insights that enable early intervention, facilitate timely support, and promote the well-being of children as they grow and develop.

**Unlocking Possibilities:**

A Practical Guide for Parents to Introduce AI and Work with It.

**Welcome to the Practical Guide for Parents:** Introducing AI and Working with It!

In today's rapidly evolving world, artificial intelligence (AI) has become an integral part of our lives, impacting various aspects of society, from education to daily routines. As parents, it's essential to navigate this AI-driven landscape and equip our children with the knowledge and skills they need to thrive in the future.

This guide aims to provide you, as a parent, with practical strategies, insights, and resources to introduce AI concepts to your children and engage with AI technology effectively. We understand that embracing AI can sometimes feel daunting or overwhelming, but rest assured, this guide is designed to make the process engaging, age-appropriate, and accessible for both you and your child.

Throughout this guide, we will explore interactive activities, age-appropriate explanations, and real-world examples to demystify AI. You will discover how to create engaging learning experiences, foster critical thinking, and encourage your child's curiosity about AI's limitless possibilities.

We will delve into topics such as the basics of AI, its benefits, potential ethical considerations, and practical ways toincorporate AI technology into your family's daily lives. From interactive experiments and storytelling to collaborative projects and educational resources, we'll cover a wide range of strategies to make learning about AI enjoyable and relatable for your child.

**Remember, this guide is not meant to make you an expert in AI, but rather to empower you with the knowledge and tools to facilitate your child's understanding and exploration of this transformative technology. By embracing AI alongside your child, you can embark on an exciting journey together, preparing them for the future while nurturing their creativity, critical thinking, and adaptability.**

**So, let's embark on this adventure, as we guide you through the fascinating world of AI and equip you with practical insights and strategies to introduce AI concepts to your child, opening doors to**

new possibilities and inspiring their curiosity every step of the way.

Let's dive in and explore the exciting realm of AI together!

# SECTION 5

# PRACTICAL APPLICATIONS AND TOOLS.

# ENGAGING PATHWAYS

A Fun and age-appropriate way to teach kids about AI and its benefits

How can parents teach their kids about artificial intelligence (AI) and its benefits in a way that is fun and right for their age?

**Start With What You Know:** Start by using simple words to describe AI, like "smart machines" or "technology that can learn." Use speech assistants or recommendation systems as examples of how AI is used in everyday life.

**Interactive Experiments:** Get kids interested in AI ideas through interactive experiments or games that are run by AI. For example, they can play with coding toys that use AI algorithms or try out apps that reply to what they do because they are powered by AI.

**Storytelling and Books:** Use books and stories that are right for their age and explain AI concepts. Find children's books with AI figures or stories about the good things AI can do for society.

**Collaborative Projects:** Get kids to work together on projects where they can learn about AI in a fun and hands-on way. This can be done by making simple robots, designing AI chatbots, or making simple AI models with computer tools that are easy for kids to use.

**Field Trips And Events:** Take advantage of chances to take kids to science museums, tech shows, or AI-related events where they can see AI in action. Interactive displays and demos can help bring the ideas to life and make them more interesting.

**Online Resources and Videos:** Look for age-appropriate online resources, videos, and learning platforms that teach AI ideas in a way that is visually interesting and easy to understand. Look for resources that are made just for kids. These resources often use graphics or game elements to make learning fun.

**Encourage Questions and Exploration:** Set up a safe place for kids to ask questions about AI and learn more about things that are related to it. Encourage their curiosity and give them chances to learn more by talking, doing experiments, or doing their own study.

Don't forget that it's important to make the plan fit the child's age and hobbies. Parents can teach their kids about AI and what it can do for them by making the learning process interactive, relevant, and fun.

# UTILIZING AI FOR INTERACTIVE AND ENGAGING SOCIAL SKILLS DEVELOPMENT IN CHILDREN.

AI technologies can be used in different ways to make social skills programs for kids that are involved and interesting. Here are some examples:

**Chatbots And Virtual Characters:** Avatars or chatbots that are run by AI can model social situations and interactions. Children can talk to these virtual figures, practice their social skills, and get feedback that is specific to them. These interactive activities offer a safe and controlled place to learn and try new things.

**Gamification:** AI can be used to make programs that teach kids social skills more fun and involved by turning them into games. AI-powered platforms can encourage children to take part and practice social skills in a fun and enjoyable way by adding game elements like rewards, challenges, and stages.

**Real-Time Feedback and Guidance:** AI systems can look at how people are interacting with each other in real time and give feedback and direction right away. AI can notice tone of voice, body language, and facial expressions, for example, and suggest ways to improve communication or reply with empathy. This feedback helps kids figure out what social cues mean and change their behavior to fit.

**Personalized Learning Paths:** AI can make sure that each child's social skills development program is made to fit their needs and skills.

By looking at a child's progress, tastes, and areas where they need to improve, AI algorithms can make personalized learning paths with tailored interventions and exercises that focus on specific social skills that need work.

**Virtual Reality (VR) and Augmented Reality (AR):** VR and AR technologies that use AI can create social situations that feel real and are engaging. Children can play in virtual world's where they can practice making friends, making choices, and seeing what happens when they do something. These models help people learn social skills by giving them hands-on experiences in a safe environment.

**Natural Language Processing (NLP):** NLP technologies that use AI can examine children's spoken and written communication skills and give them feedback. AI can help children improve their communication skills and connect with others in a positive way by pointing out grammar mistakes, unclear language, or inappropriate language use.

AI algorithms can look at data from social networks to find patterns and learn more about children's social links, ways of communicating, and social behaviors. This knowledge can help people figure out what they need to work on, make connections with their peers, and get suggestions for improving their social skills.

With these AI-powered methods, children can learn social skills in fun, interactive ways that are tailored to their specific needs. They give kids a chance to practice, get feedback, and learn in their own way, which helps them build social skills in a helpful and immersive way.

Using AI to help children learn to care about others and gain social confidence.

How can AI help kids learn to be more empathetic and understand other people's points of view?

**Empathy Training:**AI-powered programs can model empathy-related situations to help children understand and respond to the feelings of others. By looking at a person's facial expressions, tone of voice, and body language, AI can give feedback on actions related to empathy and help children learn to see things from other people's points of view.

AI algorithms can look at how people interact with each other and give personalized comments on how well people show empathy. Children can get advice on how what they say or do might affect other people and learn to see things from different points of view. This feedback makes kids more empathetic by helping them understand how their actions affect how other people feel.

**Virtual Role-Play:** Using AI, virtual settings can create simulated situations where kids can play different roles and see things from different points of view. Children can practice empathy and learn about other people's lives by connecting with virtual characters. This helps them understand and appreciate different points of view.

**Multimodal Learning:** AI can use different ways to learn about feelings and points of view, such as analyzing facial expressions, recognizing voice tones, and processing natural language. AI makes it easier for children to notice and respond to other people's emotions by using multiple sensory cues.

What role can AI-powered virtual avatars or chatbots play in helping kids build social confidence and learn how to connect with others?

AI-powered virtual images or chatbots give kids a safe place to practice interacting with other people without worrying about being judged or rejected. They can have chats, say what's on their minds, and try out different ways to talk to each other. This builds their social confidence and skills.

AI-powered virtual images or chatbots can help a child with his or her social needs in a way that is unique to that child. They can give advice, nudges, and ideas during social interactions, which can help kids handle difficult situations and learn how to communicate well.

**Real-Time Feedback:**AI-powered virtual avatars or chatbots can give comments on social interactions in real time. They can look at the child's answers, suggest ways to improve, and point out where the child does well. This feedback reinforces good actions and helps people learn how to get along better with others.

Some children may feel more comfortable engaging with virtual avatars or chatbots because they are less scary and don't put as much pressure on them as face-to-face interactions. This can make kids more interested and push them to take part in social interactions, which can help them feel better about themselves in social situations.

AI-powered virtual avatars or chatbots are always available to children, giving them constant help and chances to practice social skills. This makes it easy for kids to practice and improve their social skills at their own pace, which helps them learn better and gives them more social confidence over time.

**Real-Time Social Skills Coaching:** Using AI algorithms to give good feedback and help people get better.

By using AI-powered virtual avatars or chatbots, children can have meaningful social interactions, get personalized support and feedback, and gradually improve their social skills and confidence in a safe setting.

AI algorithms can study social situations and give children feedback in real time, which can help them improve their social skills in a number of ways:

**Natural Language Processing (NLP):** AI programs can study how people talk to each other by analyzing patterns in speech and language. They can notice conversational cues like taking turns, how relevant the topic is, and the tone of voice. They can also give comments on how to communicate more effectively. NLP algorithms can figure out if a child's speech is clear, makes sense, and is acceptable. This helps them improve their communication skill.

Computer vision techniques can be used by AI algorithms to examine how a person's face is moving. By noticing small signs like smiles, frowns, or raised eyebrows, they can figure out how someone is feeling and give feedback on how to recognize and respond to other people's feelings. This kind of feedback helps kids learn how to communicate without words and helps them develop understanding and social awareness.

**Social Context Analysis:** AI algorithms can look at how people interact with each other in certain situations, like group talks or working together on a project. They can spot patterns of participation, active listening, and adding to the talk. Children can get feedback in real time, which shows them where they can improve and encourages them to be more involved in social situations.

Sentiment analysis is when AI programs look at text or speech to figure out how a change makes someone feel. AI can give comments on how to improve communication and deal with conflicts by judging how positive, negative, or neutral interactions are as a whole. Children can learn to notice and control their feelings, which makes it easier for them to get along with others.

**Behavior Modeling:**AI algorithms can use methods from machine learning to model and predict how people will act. By looking at a lot of data about how people engage, they can figure out what works and give real-time advice on communication style, active listening, and nonverbal cues. This lets kids learn and use good social skills in their everyday contacts.

**Gamified Feedback Systems:**AI algorithms can add elements of gaming to programs that help people improve their social skills, giving instant feedback and rewards. AI-powered models or characters can act out social situations, and children can get feedback based on how well they do. Gamified feedback systems encourage kids to practice and get better at their social skills while making learning fun and interesting.

By using AI algorithms to look at social situations, children can get feedback on their social skills that are quick and tailored to them. This real-time feedback helps them learn more about themselves, shows them how to communicate effectively, and helps them keep growing and getting better at social contacts.

# AI AND THE FUTURE OF EDUCATION

Putting AI to use in the classroom Current Uses in Elementary, Middle, and High Schools and Colleges.

Artificial Intelligence (AI) is changing many parts of education and bringing about a number of exciting new ideas at different levels. Here's a look at how AI is being used in classes right now, from elementary to high school to college:

**Education in Elementary and Middle School:**

- **Personalized Learning:** Platforms that are powered by AI can adapt to the pace and style of learning of each student, making sure that the material meets their needs. These platforms can also find out where students are having trouble and give them more materials or practice to help them get better.

AI can grade multiple-choice and fill-in-the-blank tests automatically, so teachers can spend more time teaching and less time marking.

- **Learning Support Tools:** There are apps and tools that use AI to help with learning in many different areas. For example, AI tools can help you solve math problems step by step or improve your language skills.
- **Interactive Learning:** AI is also making it possible for people to learn more interactively through virtual and augmented reality. These tools can bring topics to life, making them more interesting and easier to understand.

- **Higher Education:** Advanced Research: AI can help with advanced research in higher education by sorting through large amounts of data and pointing out trends or insights that human researchers might miss.

- **Intelligent Tutoring Systems:** These systems teach and give feedback to students in a way that is similar to what a human teacher would do. They can change to meet the needs of each learner and offer customized lessons, tools, and tests.

- **Services for Students:** Many colleges use AI to improve the services they offer to students. For example, robots can answer students' questions 24 hours a day, seven days a week, and predictive analytics can help find students who may need more help or who are at risk of dropping out.

- **Course Recommendation:** AI algorithms can look at a student's past grades and goals for the future to suggest the best classes or areas of study.

These are just a few examples of how AI could be used in schooling, but there are many more. But for effective implementation, there are many things that need to be thought about carefully, such as data privacy, the quality of content, teacher training, and how to deal with possible biases in AI algorithms.

AI's possible benefits for education and the promise of personalized learning.

Artificial Intelligence (AI) has a lot of promise to make learning better.

**Here Are A Few Of The Possible Advantages:**

- **Personalized Learning:** One of the best things about AI in education is that it can help make learning more personalized. AI algorithms can figure out how a student learns, how fast they learn, and what they already know about a subject. Then, they can make educational material that fits that student's needs. Adaptive learning platforms that are powered by AI can give more difficult material to advanced learners and more help or foundational work to those who are having trouble. This personalized method meets the needs of each student in a way that makes learning more efficient and effective.

AI can automate many administrative jobs for teachers, like grading and making schedules. This gives teachers more time to teach and talk to students one-on-one. In the same way, AI tools like plagiarism checkers can quickly scan and check student entries, making the process faster and more accurate.

AI can make learning more fun and engaging, which can make students more interested in what they are doing. With the help of AI, Virtual Reality (VR) and Augmented Reality (AR) technologies can create immersive learning experiences that make themes come to life.

- **Real-Time Progress Tracking:** AI systems can track and analyze students' progress in real time, giving teachers, students, and parents useful information about learning outcomes. This can make it possible to act quickly when needed and help come up with better ideas for learning.

- **Access and Inclusion:** AI could make it easier for students who might otherwise be left out or overlooked to get an education. For example, AI-powered language translation tools can help people who don't speak English as their native language access material in their own language. Voice recognition software can help students with physical disabilities.

- **Getting Ready For The Future:** AI in education helps students get ready for a future where technology will be more and more important. It helps them get used to and better at using tools they are likely to use in college and for the job.

Even though these possible benefits sound good, it's important to think carefully about how to use AI in education to avoid problems like data privacy issues and the risk of a growing digital divide between students who have different access to technology.

# STRATEGIES FOR PARENTS TO CULTIVATE A HEALTHY SCREEN TIME

Developing a healthy balance between screen time and other activities is important for children in an AI-dominated era.Here are some strategies for parents to promote a balanced approach:

**Set Clear Screen Time Guidelines:** Establish clear and age-appropriate guidelines for screen time duration and usage. Communicate these guidelines to your children, emphasizing the importance of balance and moderation.

**Lead By Example:**Be a positive role model by demonstrating a healthy balance between screen time and other activities. Show your children the value of engaging in offline activities and spending quality time with family and friends.

**Encourage Variety in Activities:** Encourage your children to participate in a diverse range of activities beyond screens. Promote physical activities, outdoor play, hobbies, reading, creative pursuits, and face-to-face social interactions.

**Designate Tech-Free Times and Zones:** Establish specific times and zones in your home where screens are not allowed, such as during family meals, before bedtime, or in certain rooms. This helps create tech-free spaces for focused interactions and relaxation.

**Foster Family Bonding:** Create opportunities for family bonding without screens. Plan regular family activities, game nights, outings, or simply engage in conversations to strengthen family connections and reduce reliance on screens.

**Engage in Co-Viewing and Co-Playing:** Whenever possible, engage in co-viewing or co-playing with your children. This allows you to monitor their screen time, have discussions about content, and turn it into a shared experience.

**Encourage Offline Hobbies and Interests:** Support and encourage your children in pursuing offline hobbies and interests that captivate their attention and provide alternative sources of engagement and fulfillment.

**Use Screen Time as an Reward:** Make screen time contingent upon completing responsibilities or achieving goals. This helps children understand that screen time is earned and encourages a sense of balance and responsibility.

**Explore Educational and Enriching Content:** Encourage the use of screens for educational and enriching purposes. Help your children discover high-quality educational apps, interactive learning platforms, or creative tools that can enhance their skills and knowledge.

**Establish Screen-Free Bedtime Routines:** Create a screen-free bedtime routine to promote better sleep quality. Encourage reading, storytelling, or engaging in calming activities before sleep to help children wind down without screens.

Remember, the goal is not to demonize screens but to encourage a healthy balance that prioritizes a variety of activities and promotes overall well-being. Open communication, mutual understanding, and consistent reinforcement of boundaries will help children develop lifelong habits for managing screen time effectively.

**Informed Support**

Strategies for Parents to Stay Updated on AI Advancements and Better Support Their Children's Learning

Staying updated on the latest advancements and trends in AI technology is crucial for parents to better support their children's learning and exploration. Here are some strategies for parents to stay informed:

**Follow Reputable News Sources:** Regularly follow reputable news sources that cover AI-related topics. Subscribe to newsletters or RSS feeds to receive updates on the latest developments, research breakthroughs, and trends in the field of AI.

**Join AI Communities and Forums:** Engage with online communities and forums dedicated to AI. Participate in discussions, ask questions, and learn from experts and enthusiasts who can provide valuable insights and resources.

**Attend Webinars and Workshops:** Look out for webinars, workshops, and conferences related to AI. These events often provide opportunities to learn from industry experts, researchers, and practitioners who share their knowledge and experiences.

**Online Courses and MOOCs:** Explore online courses and Massive Open Online Courses (MOOCs) offered by reputable educational platforms. These courses cover various AI topics, ensuring parents stay updated with the latest advancements and techniques.

**Engage with AI Blogs and Podcasts:** Follow popular AI-focused blogs and podcasts that share insights, case studies, and interviews with experts. These platforms provide accessible and informative content that can keep parents informed about AI advancements.

**Connect with Educational Institutions:** Stay connected with educational institutions, such as universities or research centers, that have AI programs or research initiatives. Attend seminars or public lectures to gain knowledge from leading academics and researchers in the field.

**Collaborate with Educators:** Maintain open communication with your child's teachers and educators. Inquire about how AI is integrated into the curriculum and seek their guidance on educational resources or initiatives related to AI.

**Engage in Continued Learning:** Dedicate time to your own learning about AI. Read books, research papers, and academic publications to gain deeper insights into the technical aspects and societal impacts of AI.

**Explore AI-Related Organizations:** Investigate AI-related organizations and initiatives that focus on education and public awareness. These organizations often provide resources, reports, and updates on AI technology and its implications.

**Encourage Peer Learning:** Facilitate discussions and knowledge sharing among parents who are also interested in AI and its impact on education. Engage in conversations, exchange resources, and learn from each other's experiences.

By implementing these strategies, parents can stay informed about the latest advancements in AI technology. This knowledge equips them to support their children's learning and exploration, ensuring they have access to relevant resources and guidance in their AI-related pursuits.

# INSTILLING ETHICAL AWARENESS

Teaching Children about the Ethical Implications of AI in Daily Life.

Teaching children about the ethical implications of using AI in their daily lives can be an ongoing process that involves various strategies. Here are some effective approaches for parents or guardians:

**Start with The Basics:** Begin by explaining what AI is in simple terms and how it is used in different aspects of their daily lives, such as voice assistants or recommendation algorithms.

**Foster Critical Thinking**: Encourage children to ask questions and think critically about the AI systems they encounter. Help them understand that AI is created by humans and can reflect biases or limitations.

**Discuss Potential Ethical Concerns:** Engage children in conversations about the potential ethical implications of AI, such as privacy concerns, algorithmic bias, or the impact on human employment. Use real-life examples to make the concepts more relatable.

**Explore Different Perspectives:** Present various viewpoints on AI ethics to encourage children to consider different sides of the debate. These can help them develop empathy and understanding towards diverse opinions.

**Encourage Responsible Use:** Teach children to use AI technologies responsibly, emphasizing the importance of respecting privacy, seeking informed consent, and being mindful of the potential consequences of their actions.

**Promote Empathy And Fairness:** Highlight the significance of treating others fairly and with empathy, especially when it comes to AI interactions. Discuss the potential for AI to perpetuate discrimination and the importance of using technology to promote inclusivity.

**Stay Informed Together:** Keep up with the latest developments in AI ethics as a family. Engage in ongoing discussions, watch documentaries or news segments, and explore resources that address the ethical dimensions of AI.

**Involve Children In Decision-Making:** Encourage children to actively participate in family decisions related to AI usage, such as setting privacy preferences or choosing AI tools or services. This helps them develop a sense of ownership and responsibility.

**Emphasize Digital Citizenship:** Teach children about the broader concept of digital citizenship, which includes responsible use of technology, online etiquette, and respecting the rights and well-being of others in digital spaces.

**Be A Role Model:** Lead by example and demonstrate ethical behavior in your own use of AI technologies. Children often learn best by observing the actions of their parents or guardians.

Remember that teaching about AI ethics should be an ongoing dialogue, adapting to the child's age and understanding. Encourage them to ask questions, express their opinions, and explore the impact of AI in their own lives.

**Navigating Ethical Dilemmas:** Guiding Children to Make Morally Sound Decisions in Interactions with AI Technologies.

Children may encounter various ethical dilemmas when interacting with AI technologies. Here are some examples and guidance on helping them make morally sound decisions:

**Privacy Concerns:** Children may face dilemmas related to the collection and use of personal data by AI systems. Guide them to understand the importance of privacy and the potential risks associated with sharing personal information. Encourage them to make informed choices about what data they share and with whom.

**Bias and Discrimination:** AI systems can perpetuate biases or discriminate against certain groups. Teach children about the concept of fairness and help them recognize bias in AI algorithms. Encourage them to question and challenge biased outcomes, promoting inclusivity and equality.

**Ai Reliance And Autonomy:** Children may become overly dependent on AI systems, compromising their own critical thinking and decision-making abilities. Encourage them to think independently, emphasizing the importance of using AI as a tool while considering multiple perspectives and information sources.

**Accountability and Responsibility:** Children may face dilemmas regarding responsibility for AI-generated content or actions. Teach them about the consequences of their online behavior and the importance of taking responsibility for their actions, even if AI systems are involved.

**Emotional Connection to AI:** Children may develop emotional attachments to AI-powered devices or virtual assistants. Guide them to maintain a healthy distinction between AI and human relationships, helping them understand the limitations of AI and the value of genuine human connections.

**Trust and Deception:** Children may encounter AI systems designed to deceive or manipulate users. Teach them to be cautious and skeptical, promoting critical thinking and verifying information from reliable sources. Emphasize the importance of trustworthiness in AI systems and the need for transparency.

**Automation and Job Displacement**: Children may grapple with ethical dilemmas surrounding the impact of AI on employment. Discuss the potential societal implications and encourage them to think about how AI can be harnessed to create positive social and economic changes.

# FOSTERING ETHICAL AI USE

How Schools and Parent-Teacher Collaboration Help Children Learn.

Schools can teach children a lot about how to use AI in a responsible way. Here are some ways that schools can help, as well as ways that parents can work with teachers.

**Integration into Curricula:** Schools can teach about AI ethics and how to use AI in a responsible way. These can include lessons, projects, or tasks from different fields that look at the ethical implications of AI.

**Parents' Role:** Parents can support these efforts by talking to their kids about what they're learning in school, reinforcing what they've learned at home, and having conversations with them about how AI affects ethics.

**Experts And Guests Who Speak:** Students can learn a lot from hearing from guest speakers or experts in the area of AI ethics. They can talk about real-life situations, give case studies, and lead discussions to help students learn more about ethical problems.

**Role of Parents:** Parents can work with schools to find experts or people who can talk about AI ethics and what it means. They can also go to these classes to help their kids remember what they've learned and talk more with them.

**Programs for Digital Citizenship:**AI ethics can be a part of digital citizenship programs that schools can offer. Students can learn from these classes how to act responsibly online, how to think critically, and how to use AI tools and platforms in an ethical way.

**Parents' Role:** Parents can support the ideas taught in digital citizenship programs by talking to their kids about how to act responsibly online, how to protect their privacy, and how important it is to make ethical decisions when using AI. They can also help kid's use these ideas when they deal with AI every day.

**Collaborative Projects and Discussions:** Schools can help students explore the ethical aspects of AI by setting up collaborative projects and talks. This can be done through group activities, debates, or problem-solving situations that force students to think about ethics.

**Parents' Role:** Parents can help their kid's get involved in these projects by giving them advice, giving them access to resources, and getting them to think critically about ethical issues connected to AI. They can also talk about these things at home to get a better idea of them.

**Collaboration Between Parents and Teachers:** Schools can urge parents and teachers to work together to teach kids about AI ethics. This can be done through meetings between parents and teachers, workshops, or newsletters that give information, tools, and advice on how to encourage ethical use of AI.

**Role of Parents:** Parents can take part in parent-teacher meetings and training on AI ethics. They can talk to teachers about how to reinforce moral lessons at home and they can share tools or ideas they find to make the conversation richer.

**Ongoing Professional Development for Teachers:** Schools can offer teachers chances for professional development that will help them learn more about AI ethics. This will give teachers the tools they need to talk about ethics in a meaningful way in the classroom.

**Parents' Role:** Parents can show their support for teachers continuing to learn about AI ethics as part of their professional growth. They can also tell the school management how important it is to teach teachers about AI ethics as part of their training programs.

By getting parents and teachers to work together, schools can repeat lessons on how to use AI in an ethical way. If parents get involved and help with these efforts, it will make it easier for children to understand and use ethical concepts related to AI in their daily lives.

**Promoting Moral Discussion**

Getting kids to talk about AI's moral implications in an open and honest way.

For kids to understand and care about AI, it's important to have open and honest conversations with them about its social implications. Here are some things that parents can do to get their kids to talk and share their opinions:

**Create A Safe and Non-Judgmental Environment:**Set up a envi-ronment where kids can say what they think and feel without worrying about being judged. Encourage them to be open-minded and let them know that their opinions will be taken into account.

**Start Talks With:** Start conversations about AI ethics when you're doing everyday things or when the subject comes up. For example, when using AI devices or seeing AI in the media ask open-ended questions to get people talking about the ethical effects.

**Listening with Intent:** Active hearing means giving your children your full attention and showing that you care about what they have to say. Encourage them to say more about their thoughts, feelings, and worries about how AI affects ethics.

**Ask Things That Make You Think:** Ask questions that get people to think critically and reflect. For example, "How do you think AI decisions can affect people's lives?" or "Can you think of any possible biases in AI systems?"

**Talk about Different Points of View:** Bring up different points of view and social questions about AI. Talk about different points of view and look into the social issues that come up when AI is used. This helps kids learn about a subject from many different angles.

**Use Images from Real Life:** Use real-world examples of AI technologies and their ethical effects to make the talks more relatable and real. For example, you could talk about bias in AI, worries about privacy, or the effect of automation on jobs.

Encourage research and discovery. To learn more about AI ethics, encourage kids to do their own research and look at different sources of information. Tell them to look for news stories, videos, or case studies that talk about social issues related to AI.

**Model Open-Mindedness:** Show that you have an open mind by listening to different points of view and recognizing the complexity of ethical issues. Encourage respectful arguments and conversations in the family, and stress how important it is to look at things from different points of view.

Validate and respect opinions. Validate your children's opinions and urge them to think critically about the ethical issues of AI. Even if their ideas are different from yours, accept them and make a space for healthy conversation.

**Think About Ethics When Making Decisions:** Include kids in the decision-making process when AI is involved. Before they make decisions about privacy settings, data sharing, or using AI, tell them to think about the ethical effects.

# POTENTIAL DOWNSIDES AND CHALLENGES OF AI INTEGRATION IN EDUCATION

Getting rid of educational inequality and how to do it.

AI in education has a lot of possible benefits, but there are also risks and challenges that need to be thought about. Some of them are:

**Disparities In Education:** Integration of AI could make existing differences in schooling worse. Some poor towns or developing countries may not have easy access to tools and resources that use AI. This creates a digital divide. Richer schools or students who can afford better tools may benefit more than poorer schools or students, widening the gap between them.

**Bias In Algorithms:** AI systems learn from data, and if the data matches societal biases, it can make those biases even stronger. If AI systems used in education are biased, it could lead to unfair results and make stereotypes and attitudes even stronger. For example, AI algorithms might suggest certain job paths to students based on skewed data from the past, which would limit their options.

**Loss of Human Connection:** If AI is used too much in education, it could make human contact less important in the learning process. Education isn't just about giving out information; it's also about providing emotional support, mentorship, and personalized advice. If AI completely replaces human teachers, students might miss the social and emotional parts of learning that are important for their overall growth.

**Concerns About Ethics:**The use of AI brings ethical questions about privacy, data security, and consent. Collecting and analyzing a lot of student data for AI programs could put their privacy at risk and make people worried about data protection. Safeguards must be in place to make sure that student data is used in a responsible way and that AI systems used in education are clear.

These problems can be solved and educational imbalance can be reduced in the following ways:

**Making Sure Everyone has The Same Access:** Policymakers and educational institutions should work to make sure that everyone has the same access to tools and resources that use AI, especially in underserved areas. Initiatives like making technology cheaper or giving it away for free, crossing the digital divide, and working with other groups can help close the gaps.

To deal with bias and diversity, developers and researchers of AI algorithms and models used in education must put fairness, openness, and diversity at the top of their list of priorities. AI systems should be checked and evaluated regularly so that biases can be found and fixed. Diverse teams should work on the creation process to reduce bias and get a broader view.

**Balance Between Ai and Human Involvement:**AI can help improve education, but it shouldn't replace human teachers. Instead, it should work with them. A balanced method that uses both AI technology and the knowledge and guidance of teachers can make the most of both. It is very important for education to stress the value of human connection, mentorship, and emotional support.

**Setting Up Moral Guidelines:** Strong moral rules and standards should be in place to protect the privacy, security, and consent of student data. In AI systems, there should be clear rules about how to gather, store, and use student data. Regular audits and reviews can make sure that rules are followed and stop data from being misused.

By addressing these problems, stakeholders can work to use AI in education to its fullest potential while promoting fairness, inclusion, and equal chances for all learners.

**Giving Teachers More Power:** Help and training on how to use AI tools well in the classroom.

For successful integration, it is important to train and help teachers learn how to use AI tools in their classes. Here are some ways to make this happen:

**Professional Development Programs:** Schools should offer full professional development programs that focus on how AI can be used in teaching. These schools should teach teachers how to use AI tools effectively in the classroom, as well as how to use them from a technical standpoint. Workshops, seminars, and online training can be used to help teachers learn and get better at what they do.

**Joint Learning Communities:** Educators can share best practices and experiences more easily when they are part of joint learning communities. Setting up platforms or places where teachers can connect, work together, and share ideas about how AI can be used can help create a supportive environment for learning and growth that lasts. Peer coaching and networking are also good ways for educators to build their confidence and skills.

**Accessible Resources and Toolkits:** Educators' professional growths can be helped by making AI-related resources and toolkits easy to find and use. Some of these resources are teaching materials, lesson plans, case studies, and tips on how to use specific AI tools in the real world. These kinds of tools can be found in curated repositories, online libraries, or dedicated websites.

**Ongoing Technical Support:** Educators should be able to get help with any problems or hurdles they run into while using AI tools. Help desks, online forums, and helplines run by AI experts or support staff can provide help and troubleshooting in a timely manner. This help should be responsive, personalized, and made to fit the wants of each educator.

**Collaboration with Ai Experts:** It can be very helpful to encourage trainers and AI experts or researchers to work together. Through partnerships with universities, research institutions, or industry professionals, you can learn about the latest AI technologies and how they can be used in teaching. Collaboration on projects, study, or guest lectures can help teachers learn more about AI tools and come up with new ways to teach.

**Reflective Practice And Evaluation:** Teachers should use reflective practice to figure out how well AI is working in their classes. Encouragement of self-reflection, getting feedback from students, and constant evaluation can help teachers figure out where they can improve and make their teaching methods better. For AI integration strategies to change and get better, there needs to be a mindset of reflection and learning from experiences.

**Help with Policy and Money:** Policymakers and educational organizations should make AI integration in education a top priority by making policies that support it and giving enough money for it. This includes spending money on infrastructure, giving people access to AI tools and resources, and giving people a reason to work on their professional growth. A policy-friendly setting can inspire teachers and set the stage for a successful implementation.

By using these strategies, teachers can gain the skills, knowledge, and confidence they need to use AI tools in their classrooms successfully. Support, teamwork, and a focus on reflective practice can help teachers use AI technology to its fullest potential and improve their students' learning.

# INSTILLING EMPATHY, COMPASSION, AND PRIVACY VALUES IN FAMILIES.

To help kid's make morally good choices, it's important to support open communication, promote critical thought, and teach values like empathy, fairness, and respect. Engage them in conversations, show them ethical situations, and ask them to think about how their decisions will affect others. By teaching children the right skills and giving them a sense of right and wrong, they will be able to handle ethical issues that arise from AI technologies.

**Striking a Balance**

Taking advantage of AI's benefits while teaching kids about empathy, compassion, and privacy.

A family needs to think carefully about how to balance the benefits of AI with teaching ideals like empathy, compassion, and respect for privacy. Here are some ways to get that mix right:

**Open Communication:** Encourage your family to talk about AI in an open and constant way. Encourage people to talk about its pros, possible cons, and social issues. This conversation will help family members come to a common idea and encourage them to think critically.

**Set Up Clear Rules:**Set clear rules and limits for how everyone in the family can use AI technologies. Set limits on screen time, private settings, and access to AI tools based on a person's age. Make sure that these rules fit with the values of the family and the wants of the children as they grow.

**Show Understanding And Kindness:** Show empathy and compassion in your own online and offline contacts. Encourage family members to take these values with them when they deal with AI systems and be kind and respectful to virtual entities.

# INTRODUCTION TO SPECIAL NEEDS EDUCATION

A look at the many kinds of special needs and learning disabilities.

Autism Spectrum Disorder (ASD) is a developmental disorder that changes the way a person interacts with others, talks, and acts. People with ASD may have trouble with social skills, understanding sensory information, and doing the same things over and over again.

**Attention-Deficit/Hyperactivity Disease**(ADHD): ADHD is an neurodevelopmental disease that causes people to be impulsive, have trouble paying attention, and move around a lot. People with ADHD may have trouble focusing, staying organized, and controlling their impulses.

**Specific Learning Disabilities (SLD):** People with SLD have trouble learning in certain areas, like reading, writing, or math. Some common examples are dyslexia, which is trouble reading, dysgraphia, which is trouble writing, and dyscalculia, which is trouble with math.

**Intellectual Disability (ID):** People with ID have trouble thinking and behaving in ways that help them get along with others. People with ID may have trouble with thinking, getting along with others, and doing things.

Speech and language disorders make it hard to talk and understand what other people are saying. They can also make it hard to share thoughts and ideas.

**Sensory Processing Disorder (SPD):** is a condition in which it is hard to react to and process sensory information. People with SPD May be too sensitive or not sensitive enough to sensory input, which can make it hard for them to go about their daily lives.

Emotional and behavioral disorders are things like oppositional defiant disorder (ODD), conduct disorder (CD), and mood disorders that make it hard to control feelings and behaviors.

**Developmental Coordination Disorder (DCD):** Also, called dyspraxia, DCD affects both fine and gross movement skills and coordination. People with DCD may find it hard to do things that require balance, like writing, tying their shoes, or playing sports.

**Visual or Hearing Impairments:** Visual impairments, like blindness or low vision, and hearing impairments can make it hard to learn and need special help and adjustments.

Traumatic Brain Injury, or TBI, is brain loss caused by a traumatic event. Depending on which part of the brain is damaged, it can cause a range of mental, physical, and emotional problems.

It's important to remember that everyone with special needs or anlearning disability is different, and that their problems can have different effects and be of different levels of seriousness. It's important to give each person the help, accommodations, and interventions they need to meet their particular needs and help them learn and grows.

**How Can Ai Help Make Sure That Kids With Special Needs Get A Personalized And Inclusive Education?**

AI can help kids with special needs get a more personalized and inclusive education in a big way. Here's why it's important to use AI in this situation:

**Customized Learning Experiences:** AI algorithms can look at a huge amount of data, such as a person's learning profile, their tastes, and how well they are doing, to make learning experiences that are unique to each person. By using AI, teachers can change the way they teach, the content they use, and the tasks they do to fit the needs and skills of each child with special needs. This personalization helps them learn more and makes them feel like they own their education.

**Adaptive And Interactive Support:** Learning platforms that are driven by AI can change the level of difficulty and speed of lessons based on how well a child is doing. These platforms can give real-time feedback, prompts, and ideas that can help children with special needs deal with problems and learn important skills. Also, AI technologies that are interactive, like virtual assistants or chatbots, can connect with students, answer their questions, and help them, making their learning experience better.

**Accessibility And Arrangements:** AI can make it easier for children with special needs to get what they need by making arrangements for them. Text-to-speech and voice recognition are two technologies that can help students who have trouble reading or writing. Visual recognition systems that are driven by AI can help people who can't see by telling them what things look like. By using AI to make learning materials accessible, children with special needs can fully take part in the learning process and get to the materials in a way that works for them.

**Data-Driven Decision Making:** Artificial intelligence makes it possible to gather and analyze a lot of data about special needs education. This information can be used to find patterns, track growth, and help make decisions. Educators can use AI-generated insights to make smart changes to teaching methods, interventions, and accommodations, making sure that children with special needs get the best help.

**Individualized Intervention and Therapy:** AI can help make sure that children with special needs get individualized interventions and treatments. For example, virtual reality platforms that are powered by AI can build immersive environments to help people learn social skills or simulate real-life situations to help with behavior therapy. AI can look at how a child responds and acts during therapy meetings. This gives therapists important information they can use to make treatment plans and track progress.

**Teamwork and Communication:**AI-powered teamwork tools can help teachers, therapists, and parents of a child with special needs talk to each other and work together. These tools can make it easier for people to share information, track progress, and set goals, making sure that everyone is on the same page and working together to help the child grow.

By putting AI into personalized and inclusive education, children with special needs can get individualized help, better access, data-driven decision making, individualized assistance, and better teamwork. AI technologies have the ability to change how children with special needs learn, grow, and reach their fullest potential.

# AI AND WELL-BEING:

We will talk about ways to keep a good relationship with technology and look at how AI might affect children's mental health and well-being.

AI can have a big effect on the mental health and general well-being of children. Here is a look at the possible effects of AI on health and happiness, as well as ways to keep a good relationship with technology:

**Emotional Support:** Chatbots, virtual companions, and therapy apps that are driven by AI can help with stress, anxiety, and other mental health problems. These tools give kids a safe place to talk about their feelings, get advice, and try out ways to deal with them. But it's important to keep in mind that AI shouldn't replace human help. Instead, it should be used along with professional advice when it's needed.

**Personalization and Self-Reflection:** AI can make learning situations more relevant to each person and help them see their strengths and where they can improve. By knowing how they learn and what they're good at, kids can develop a sense of self-awareness and self-reflection, which is good for their growth and health.

**Mindfulness and Well-being Apps:** Mindfulness and well-being apps that are driven by AI can help kids learn how to meditate, relax, and deal with stress. These apps can help people stay healthy and keep their lives in balance by giving them reminders, tips, and personalized ideas.

**Digital Detox and Healthy Technology Habits:** It's important to develop healthy technology habits so you don't spend too much time in front of a screen and have a good mix of online and offline activities. Encourage people to take regular breaks from screens, set up places or times when they can't use their devices, and get them involved in physical activities, hobbies, and face-to-face interactions. These can help them stay healthy generally.

**Critical Thinking and Media Literacy:** Teaching kids how to think critically and how to use the media can help them find their way through the huge amount of information available on platforms powered by AI. By teaching children to be smart and able to judge sources, they can better understand and control how AI-generated material might affect their well-being.

**Getting Parents Involved and Keeping An Eye On:** When it comes to AI, parents are very important to the well-being of their children. Open conversation, setting limits, and keeping an eye on what kids do online can help keep them safe and make sure they use AI technology in a healthy way.

**Concerns About Ethics And Digital Health:** Teaching kids about the moral implications of AI and encouraging them to use technology in a responsible way can be good for their general health. Talking to kids about things like privacy, consent, and the effects of algorithms can help them make smart choices and manage the digital world in a responsible way.

It's important to remember that even though AI can provide useful tools and help, children still need to meet with real people and have real conversations. To improve children's mental health and well-being as a whole, it is important to find a balance between the benefits of AI and good ways to use technology.

# SECTION 6

# NURTURING FUTURE READY MINDS

# EXPLORING HOW AI CAN INSPIRE CREATIVITY AND INNOVATION.

We are looking into how AI can help kids be more creative and come up with new ideas when they are doing things like making music, drawing, or sharing stories.

AI could help kid's be more creative and innovative in their artistic work by giving them new tools, resources, and opportunities. AI can help kids in the following ways when it comes to artistic arts:

**Composing Music:**AI can help kid's write music by giving them clever tools for writing music. For example, AI systems can make musical suggestions based on melodies or harmonies that are given. This can help children try out new musical ideas. AI-powered platforms can also offer virtual instruments that kids can use to try out different sounds and combinations, even if they don't have access to real instruments.

**Visual Arts:**AI can help kids with their visual arts by giving them tools for making digital art. AI algorithms can make things like automatic coloring, style transfer, and image generation possible. This lets kids try out different art styles and methods. AI-powered platforms can also give kids virtual boards and tools for 3D modeling or animation, so they can try out new ways to be creative and explore their interests.

**Storytelling:**AI can help and inspire children when they are trying to tell stories. AI-powered platforms can give story ideas, come up with characters, and even help kids write stories based on what they like. By using AI, kids can try out different story frameworks, plot points, and ways to tell a story, which helps them develop their imagination and storytelling skills.

**Collaborative Art Projects:** AI can help kids work together on art projects. AI-powered platforms can bring together kids from different places so they can work on art projects together. These platforms can give you tool for real-time collaboration, feedback mechanisms, and engaging interfaces, which can help your team work together, talk to each other and come up with new ideas.

**Creative Learning Resources:** AI can provide creative learning resources that are personalized and engaging. Educational apps or platforms that are powered by AI can give kid's tutorials, interactive lessons, and feedback that is based on their skill level and hobbies. AI can match the level of effort and content to a child's progress by using adaptive learning algorithms. This keeps the child interested and gives them a challenge in their artistic pursuits.

**Artistic Exploration and Discovery:** AI can help kids learn about different kinds of art. Based on what a child likes, AI-powered recommendation systems can suggest artworks, music compositions, or books. This broadens their creative tastes and introduces them to different cultures and styles. AI can act as a guide and curator, showing kids new artists, genres, and art trends.

It's important to remember that AI can give you useful tools and resources, but it shouldn't replace the value of real-world experiences, mentorship, and artistic discovery. AI should be seen as a way to help children develop their creativity by pushing them to try new things, take risks, and find their own artistic voices.

## AI and Getting Better

We will look at how AI can help with personal growth and well-being outside of schooling, such as with tools for self-reflection, setting goals, and personal development.

AI can play a big role in getting kids to be more active, tracking their movements, and giving them better sports training. Here are a few ways that AI can help with physical education:

**Tracking And Keeping An Eye On Activity:** Wearable devices with AI, like fitness trackers, can keep track of how active a child is, including how many steps they take, how far they walk, and how many calories they burn. These devices can give kid's real-time feedback, motivational nudges, and rewards to encourage them to stay busy and do physical activities regularly.

**Movement Analysis and Correction:** AI can look at how people move and give comments to help people get better at sports and avoid getting hurt. For example, AI algorithms can look at how a child runs, shoots a basketball, or swings a golf club and make ideas for how to improve in real time. This feedback can help kids learn how to move correctly and improve their ability in different sports.

**Virtual Coaching and Training:** AI-powered virtual coaching platforms can give children in different sports personalized training plans and directions. These platforms can offer interactive tutorials, workout plans, and training events that are made for a child's age, skill level, and goals. AI algorithms can change the training based on how well the child is doing. This makes sure that the child is pushed in the right way and moves forward at his or her own pace.

**Gamification of Physical Activity:** AI can turn physical activities into games, which will make them more fun and interesting for kids. Fitness apps or interactive games that are driven by AI can create virtual challenges, competitions, and rewards to get kids to do more physical activities. By adding play, stories, and making goals, AI can make kids more interested in and able to stick with physical activity.

**Injury Prevention and Rehabilitation:** AI can help find possible injury risks and give advice on how to avoid injuries and get better from them. AI algorithms can look at data about how people move, find imbalances or weaknesses, and offer exercises or other ways to fix these problems. AI-powered platforms can also provide kids with tools and educational materials that teach them how to avoid injuries and train safely.

**Adaptive Physical Education:** AI can make it possible for children with different skills and needs to take part in adaptive physical education programs. AI algorithms can make plans, changes, and accommodations for physical activities based on each person's skills and goals. This method makes it possible for kids with disabilities or special needs to take part in physical education and sports in a way that is meaningful and helpful.

It is important to make sure that safety, privacy, and social concerns are put first when AI is used in physical education. AI technologies should be made with the help of experts in physical education, coaches, and medical workers to make sure they are useful and safe. Also, it's important to find a balance between the use of AI technology and helping children connect with people, get involved in their communities, and enjoy physical activities.

## AI and Making Moral Choices for Parents

Discussing the ethical issues that parents should think about when using AI to help them raise their children and giving advice on how to make ethically sound decisions.

Parents must be aware of and think about a number of social issues when using AI to help them raise their children. Here are some important things to remember:

**Privacy and The Safety of Data:** When their kid uses AI technologies, parents should put the privacy and safety of their child's data first. It is important to choose AI systems or devices that have a good reputation and can be trusted, and that follow strict data protection rules. Parents should also know how the information is kept, used, and shared, and they should be happy with how much control they have over their child's data.

**Informed Consent:** When using AI technologies that collect or share data, parents should think about how well they have gotten their child's informed consent, especially if the child is old enough to understand what's going on. Open and honest communication with the child about the use of AI technologies can help build trust and make sure they feel valued and included in the decision-making process.

**Bias and Fairness:** Parents should be aware of the fact that AI systems can have biases. AI systems are only as fair as the data they are taught on, so if the data is skewed or doesn't have a lot of variety, it can lead to biased results. Parents should look for AI tools that actively deal with bias and make sure that the tools they use don't promote discrimination or stereotypes.

**Human Supervision and Judgment:** AI technologies can give useful insights and help, but they shouldn't replace human supervision and judgment. AI tools can help parents in addition to their own knowledge, experience, and gut feelings. It's important to keep in mind that AI systems have their limits and may not always understand all the details of complicated scenarios.

**Emotional And Social Growth:** Parents should be wary of how AI devices might affect their child's emotional and social growth. Too much dependence on AI for emotional support or social interactions could hurt the development of social skills, empathy, and human connections. It is important to find a balance between how AI helps and how it helps people.

**Transparency And The Ability To Explain:** Parents should try to find AI technologies that are clear and easy to explain. It's important to know how AI systems decide what to do, make suggestions, or give insights. Parents should be able to get clear explanations and be able to understand and evaluate the information given by AI tools so they can make choices about their child's well-being that are based on facts.

**Continuous Assessment and Adaptation:** When AI is used, ethical concerns mean that it needs to be constantly evaluated and changed. As technology changes, it's important for parents to keep up with the latest news, study, and best practices. To keep up with changing social norms and values, it is important to regularly reevaluate the ethical effects of using AI for parenting.

Parents can use AI technologies in a responsible and ethical way that puts their child's well-being and best interests first by being aware of these ethical concerns and making well-informed decisions.

# UNCOVERING INSIGHTS AND ENHANCING SOCIAL SKILLS:

**The Power of Social Network Analysis Driven by AI.**

AI algorithms can look at data from social networks to find trends and learn more about how children connect with each other and communicate.

**Network Mapping:**AI systems can look at how children in a social network are connected and how they are related to each other. By looking at how people know each other, how they talk to each other, and how often they talk to each other, AI can make visual representations of the network, highlighting important ties and finding social clusters.

**Communication Analysis:** AI systems can look at what children say and how they talk to each other on social networks. This means looking at how often, how long, what they talk about, and how they talk, such as through text messages or phone calls. By processing and analyzing this data, AI can figure out how and what kids like to talk about in general.

**Sentiment Analysis:** AI systems can figure out how children feel about what they say on social networks by analyzing the emotional tone and tone of voice. AI can figure out if a conversation is generally positive, negative, or neutral by looking at the words used, such as keywords, mood indicators, and contextual clues. This study shows how people feel about each other in the network.

**Influence and Leadership Identification:** AI algorithms can look at communication patterns, network centrality, and engagement levels to find important people or leaders in a social network. By figuring out who the key influencers are, AI can show who may have a big effect on how the group works and how people connect with each other.

**Behavior Patterns:** AI algorithms can look at activity levels, participation rates, and reaction times to see how people act in a social network. By looking at how children use and interact with the network, AI can find specific patterns of behavior that may affect social ties and how people talk to each other.

**Social Skill Assessment:** AI systems can use data from social networks to figure out how social skills are. AI can help us understand where children's social skills are strong and where they need to improve by comparing their communication patterns and interactions to known social skill benchmarks.

By using AI algorithms to look at social network data, patterns and ideas about how children make friends and talk to each other can be found. These insights can help find places to improve, guide interventions, encourage good social interactions, and, in the end, help children develop their social skills.

Educators and parents can use social network analysis to help children improve their social skills and positive social behaviors.

Teachers and parents can use what they learn from social network analysis to help children improve their social skills and behave well with others in a number of ways:

**Targeted Interventions:** Educators and parents can make targeted interventions to help with specific social skills needs by knowing the social connections and communication patterns that come out of social network analysis. They can give each child the help, coaching, or tools they need to improve their social skills in areas where they may be struggling.

**Peer Group Formation:** Social network analysis can help find potential peer groups or social clusters based on similar hobbies, communication patterns, or common goals. Educators and parents can use this information to help kids form peer groups that are helpful and open to everyone. By helping kid's make friends in these groups, they can practice and improve their social skills in a safe and interesting setting.

**Opportunities to Be A Mentor:** A social network analysis can point out important people or leaders in a social network. Teachers and parents can put kids in touch with these role models, which can lead to mentoring relationships. Mentors can give advice, be good social models, and help kids improve their social skills by interacting with them and watching them.

**Feedback and Direction:** Educators and parents can give specific feedback and direction to children based on what they learn from social network research. They can point out good ways of communicating, encourage social behaviors that are wanted, and talk about things that could be better. This feedback can be made to fit the needs of each person and given in a positive and helpful way.

**Social Skills Training Programs:** Social network analysis can help with how social skills training programs are made and how they are used. Educators and parents can use these insights to focus on specific areas of social skill development, tailor interventions to the needs of individual children or groups of children, and judge the success of programs based on changes in the way social networks work.

**Promoting Good Online Behavior:** Social network analysis can give us information about how and with whom children engage online. This knowledge can help teachers and parents talk to their kids about being responsible online, being a good digital citizen, and communicating in the right way. They can help kids keep their online interactions positive and respectful, creating a safe and helpful digital world.

By using what they learn from social network analysis, teachers and parents can give targeted help, make social settings more welcoming, offer mentorships, give feedback and advice, create programs to teach social skills, and encourage positive social behavior both online and offline. Together, these tactics help kids learn how to get along with others and help them handle social situations well.

# BOOSTING COLLABORATION AND PROBLEM-SOLVING: THE POWER OF AI-INFUSED GAMIFIED LEARNING PLATFORMS FOR POSITIVE SOCIAL INTERACTIONS

**Equal Participation and Inclusion:** AI programs can make sure that every child in a virtual collaborative setting has the same chance to take part and contribute. AI can stop strong people from taking over by getting everyone involved and making sure everyone gets a turn. This makes the place a better place for everyone to work together.

**Teamwork and Communication Skills:** In virtual collaborative settings, kids can learn how to work as a team and talk to each other. When kids work on projects and tasks together, they learn how to work together, give out tasks, and talk about their ideas. People can work well together and have useful conversations with the help of tools that are powered by AI.

**Thinking critically and Solving Problems:** Virtual collaborative environments that are powered by AI often include activities that require critical thought to solve problems. Children work together to figure out how to solve problems and make decisions based on what they know. When they are needed, AI programs can give hints or ideas. This helps people solve problems by getting them to think critically and work together.

**Improved Peer Feedback And Learning:**AI systems can make it easier for people to give and receive feedback when they work together in a virtual setting. Children can give their friends helpful feedback on their work by suggesting ways to make it better. Peer-to-peer feedback is a way for everyone to learn, improve, and keep improving.

**Reflection And Iteration:**AI-powered virtual collaborative spaces can make it easier for people working on group projects to think about what they've done and make changes. Children can look at their old work, decide how well they worked together, and make changes based on what other people say and what they see. People are forced to think about themselves, be flexible, and keeplearning through this process.

Overall, AI-powered virtual collaborative environments give kids a place to learn together; work on their teamwork and communication skills, and develop an sense of shared responsibility. By using AI, these learning environments help kids work together and get along better, which prepares them for future group projects and jobs in the real world.

**How to Get People to Work Better Together and Solve Problems:** How Powerful Are AI-Infused Game-based learning platforms to help people get along well with each other

AI-powered gamified learning tools can help kids get along and work together to solve problems in a number of ways:

Challenges, rewards, and leaderboards are all parts of gaming that get kids more interested and involved in learning. Based on how each child is doing, AI algorithms can change the level of effort and the content. This makes sure that each child is challenged just enough.

This makes it easier for people to get along with each other and encourages them to do things where they have to work together to solve problems.

**Teamwork and Working Together:** In gamified learning platforms, there are a lot of jobs that require kids to work together as a team to reach the same goals. AI programs can make it easier to form a team, get people to work together, and give each person a job so that everyone can take part. Kids learn how to work as a team, how to speak well, and how important it is to work together to solve problems through these group activities.

**Peer Learning And Healthy Competition:** Using AI in gamified learning tools can help kids compete with each other in a healthy way. Leaderboards and awards can show how far each person or team has come, which can encourage friendly competition. This game helps kids learn from each other because they can watch how their peers solve problems and use strategies and learn from that. This helps build a group of learners who help each other and work together.

**Personalized Learning Paths:** AI systems can look at each person's success data and make learning paths that are best for them. Game-based learning tools can make the challenges and activities fit each child's skills, weaknesses, and way of learning. This personalized method lets kids work together on tasks that are right for their skill levels. This gives them a sense of independence and competence when fixing problems together.

**Learning by Doing and Getting Feedback Right Away:** Gamified learning tools that are powered by AI can give kids immediate feedback on how they try to solve problems. AI programs can look at their answers and tell them how to improve or how to do things differently. This real-time feedback allows for iterative learning, in which children can work together to improve how they solve problems and learn from their mistakes. This makes them more resilient and open to change.

**Peer Support and Recognition from Others:** Social features like chat rooms or message boards can be added to gamified learning platforms so that kids can talk to each other and help each other when they are working together to solve a problem. Peer recognition tools, like likes, comments, and virtual rewards, can help peers have better social interactions, work together, and feel like they've done something.

Gamified learning platforms make learning fun and interactive by mixing gamification and AI technologies. This helps people get along with each other and pushes them to work together to solve problems. These tools encourage kids to work together, help each other, learn in a way that works for them, get feedback right away, and ask their peers for help. In the end, this helps them grow as people and as thinkers.

# FOSTERING COLLABORATIVE EXPERIENCES:

People can work together better with the help of tools for interactive storytelling, coding, and virtual reality that are powered by AI.

**Storytelling With Twist Ai Drives It:** AI-powered platforms for interactive storytelling let kid's help make up stories by acting out different parts and making choices that change the story. AI programs are used on these platforms to change the plot based on what each user does. This gives the impression that everyone is helping to tell the story. Through this process, kids learn to work together, argue, and make decisions as a group.

**Platforms for Collaborative Coding:** AI runs these platforms, which let kid's work on coding projects together, share code snippets, and give each other feedback. On these sites, AI algorithms make it easier to review code, suggest changes, and get people to work together on coding jobs. Children can work on code projects together, learn from each other's ideas, and improve their problem-solving and teamwork skills.

**Virtual Reality (VR) Experiences that People Do Together:** AI-powered virtual reality platforms can make it possible for kids to work on projects and activities together in a way that feels real. Kids can use images to talk to each other and connect to virtual worlds. They can also work together to solve problems in these worlds. People can work together and talk to each other better in a virtual setting when they do these things.

# EXPLORING HOW AI CAN PROVIDE INSIGHTS AND TOOLS TO ENHANCE PARENTS.

We are looking into how AI can help parents understand how their child feels and give them ideas and tools to help their kid grow emotionally.

It's important to understand and supports a child's mental growth for their overall health and growth. With improvements in artificial intelligence (AI), parents may be able to use technology to figure out how their child is feeling and help them in the right way. AI can help parents understand their children and help them grow mentally in the following ways:

**Emotion Recognition:** Artificial intelligence can be used to make systems that can read and understand facial expressions, voice tones, and other non-verbal signs of emotions. AI programs can tell parents a lot about how their child is feeling by looking at these signs, such as whether the child is happy, sad, angry, or scared. With this information, parents can figure out better ways to deal with their child's thoughts.

**Behavior Monitoring:** Tools powered by AI can keep track of how a child acts over time and watch how they act. AI programs can find deviations or changes in behavior, like sleep patterns, activity levels, or social interactions that could be signs of mental distress or well-being. This information can give parents the tools they need to spot possible mental problems early and take the right steps.

AI systems can figure out how a child feels about what he or she says or writes by looking at text or speech data. Parents can learn about their child's mental health by reading their chats, emails, or posts on social media, such as what worries them, what causes them stress, or what makes them happy. With this knowledge, parents can have deeper conversations and help their kids in more specific ways.

AI-powered systems can make recommendations based on what an individual child needs mentally. Parents can support their child's emotional development with the help of AI algorithms that suggest tasks, tools, or strategies based on the child's age, interests, and emotional profile. These ideas can be books, games, or chores that are meant to improve emotional intelligence and overall health.

**Chatbots And Other Online Helpers:** AI-powered virtual assistants or chatbots can help parents all the time by giving them information, resources, and ideas about how their child's feelings are changing. These assistants can talk, answer questions, and give advice on different parts of mental health. They can also show parents how to deal with tough situations.

**Visualizing Data and Getting Insights:** AI can help parents understand how their kids feel by showing them pictures and giving them information they can use. By showing data in a clear and easy-to-understand way, AI systems can point out patterns, trends, or possible areas of concern. This gives parents a fuller picture of how their child's feelings are changing and helps them decide when to step in or get help from a professional.

AI is not a replacement for human interaction, empathy, or skilled advice. It can help parents understand their kids and help them grow mentally, but it shouldn't be used instead of those things. AI technologies should be used to help parents learn more about their children and help them support their mental health in more specific ways.

**AI and How Brains Are Different**

How can AI help people with autism, ADHD, or other brain differences get the help they need and be a part of society?

AI has the potential to make big changes in how neurodiverse people are included and helped by handling their unique needs and giving them personalized help. AI can help in the following ways:

**Help with Communication:**People with autism and other brain differences often find it hard to talk to others and get along with them. AI can help people talk better with each other by giving them more ways to say what they want to say. For example, there are apps that use visual symbols or text-to-speech technology to help people who have trouble speaking or understanding language get their thoughts and needs across. AI can also help people learn how to get along with other people by creating virtual settings that look and feel like real life. This gives people a safe, controlled place to practice and improve their social skills.

AI can be used to make learning situations work for people with different types of brains. AI algorithms can change a person's curriculum and training methods to meet their needs by figuring out how they learn, what their cognitive skills and flaws are, and how they learn best. This personalized way can get people more interested, help them remember what they've learned, and improve their overall learning.

**Support for The Senses:** For example, many people with neurodiversity are sensitive to loud noises or bright lights. By watching and changing how the senses are used in real time, AI can help make settings that are easy on the senses. For example, AI-powered smart home systems can change the lighting, temperature, and sound levels automatically to fit each person's preferences. This makes the house a nicer and more useful place to be.

**Emotional Regulation and Help:** AI-powered tools can help neurodiverse people deal with stress and control their emotions. For example, wearable devices with AI algorithms can track physiological cues like heart rate or skin conductance to look for signs of worry or stress. When a big change is found, the AI system can offer personalized help, like breathing exercises or ways to calm down, to help keep feelings in check and reduce anxiety.

**Assistive Technologies:** AI can help people with neural differences do everyday jobs and tasks. For example, AI-powered virtual helpers can help people who have trouble with executive functioning, like those with ADHD, by giving them reminders, visual schedules, and step-by-step instructions. People can be more independent and get more done with these tools because they make it easier to organize, keep track of time, and finish jobs.

**Data-driven Insights:** AI can look at a lot of data to find trends and connections that have to do with neurodiversity. This study can help us find out more about differences in how people think, which could lead to new ways to help people and new treatments, therapies, and ways to help people. AI can also help find early signs of neurodiverse diseases by looking at data about how people act or how their bodies work. This means that people can get help and support faster.

It's important to keep in mind that AI should always be used in a way that respects each person's privacy, agreement, and freedom. AI systems for people with neurodiversity should be made in close collaboration with the neurodiversity group. These will make sure that their unique thoughts and experiences are taken into account when designing and putting the plan into action. AI shouldn't be thought of as a way to replace human touch, empathy, and personalized care for neurodiverse people. Instead, it should be seen as a way to add to and support these things.

# AI AND PARENT-CHILD BONDING

## AI and Parent-Child Relationships

We are looking into how AI technologies can help parents and children spend more valuable time together through shared activities, stories, and interactive experiences.

Through shared activities, stories, and engaging experiences, AI technologies can help parents and children spend more time together and get to know each other better. Here are some ways that AI can help parents and children bond:

**Engaging Storytelling:** Storytelling platforms or apps that use AI can get both kids and adults involved in engaging stories. These platforms can have engaging stories, characters that you can interact with, and stories that go in different directions, so that parents and children can work together to make and explore stories. Parents and children can bond, encourage creativity, and improve their communication skills by sharing stories together.

**SharedGaming Experiences:** Interactive games that are driven by AI can give parents and children the chance to play together. Whether they are group games, puzzles, or virtual reality experiences, these games can help people work together, talk to each other, and have fun. When a parent and child play together, they can make memories that will last and grow closer to each other.

**Virtual Experiences and Exploration:** AI can make it possible for parents and children to discover virtual worlds together. Virtual reality (VR) or augmented reality (AR) apps can take families to new places, different times in history, or fictional world's where they can share journeys and explore together. By doing these virtual activities together, parents and kids can share feelings of wonder, interest, and discovery.

**Collaborative Creativity:** AI can help parents and children work together to come up with new ideas. Platforms that are driven by AI can offer tools for making art, music, or other creative projects together. For example, parents and kids can use AI tools to make songs, create virtual art, or work together on digital stories. This way of working together helps people be creative, talk to each other, and feel like they've accomplished something together.

**Personalized Activity Suggestions:** AI can make suggestions for activities that both parents and children will enjoy. AI-powered platforms can look at the likes and dislikes of both adults and children to come up with ideas for activities, trips, or hobbies that the whole family can enjoy. Parents and children can grow closer to each other and have more meaningful moments together by doing things that they both like.

**Support and Insights for Parents:** AI technologies can offer support and insights for parents, letting them spend more quality time with their kids. Apps or devices that are powered by AI can give advice, ideas, and reminders about age-appropriate activities, encourage good parenting habits, and help parents and children bond. By using AI to improve how parents do their jobs, they can have more focused, important conversations with their kids.

AI technologies can help people connect and share experiences, but they should never replace the value of real human interaction, empathy, and quality time. AI should be seen as a tool that can improve and add to the relationship between a parent and a child by giving them more chances to connect, explore, and have fun together. The key is to find a balance between using AI technologies and making real links with real people.

# PATHWAYS TO THE FUTURE:

Finding out about jobs in AI and helping kids do well in school.

As AI keeps getting better, more and more job opportunities are opening up in this area. Helping kid's get jobs in AI-related fields can be done in the following ways:

**AI Research and Development:** Tell kid's they should go into AI research and development as a job. This means working on cutting-edge technologies, making AI programs, and helping to improve the abilities of AI. Machine learning, natural language processing, computer vision, and robotics are all exciting fields where study and new ideas can happen.

**Data Science and Analytics:** Stress how important it is to have skills in data science and analytics. AI needs a lot of data, and people who know how to gather, analyze, and draw conclusions from data are in high demand. Encourage kids to learn how to work with data, analyze statistics, and use machine learning to do well in this area.

**AI Engineering and Software Development:** Help kids find jobs in AI engineering and software development. These people create and build AI systems, put machine learning models into action, and build applications that use AI. To be successful in this area, you need to know how to use programming languages, algorithms, and software engineering.

**Ethical AI Design and Governance:** Make sure people know how important it is to think about ethics when making AI. In ethical AI design and governing careers, you make sure that AI systems are fair, open, and answerable to people. In this area, people help make AI policies, deal with bias and discrimination, and make sure AI is used in an ethical way.

**AI in Certain Fields:** Tell kids to look into how AI is used in certain fields, like healthcare, banking, cybersecurity, and agriculture. Experts in these fields need to know how to use AI methods tWhen children combine their kwith AI skills, can make a big difference in many areas.

Parents and Teachers Can Do The Following Things to Help Kid's Get Good Jobs in Ai-Related Fields:

**STEM Education Should Be Pushed:** STEM (science, technology, engineering, and math) schooling should be emphasized. Strong foundations in these areas give you the skills and knowledge you need for jobs related to artificial intelligence (AI).

**Foster Curiosity and Problem-Solving Skills:** Help kids be interested in new things and learn how to solve problems. AI needs people who can think creatively, analyze critically and solve difficult problems.

Encourage computational thinking by teaching kids how to solve problems by breaking them down, organizing data, and making programs. Computational thought helps people understand the ideas and methods of AI.

**Give Kids Access to Tools and Training:** Make sure that kids can use AI tools, online classes, coding platforms, and AI development tools. Get them involved in AI projects, competitions, and classes so they can learn by doing.

AI is a field that involves many different areas of study. Encourage kids to work with other kids who come from different fields, like computer science, math, psychology, or social studies. Interdisciplinary learning helps people see things from many different angles and think of new ideas.

**Develop Soft Skills:** Along with technical skills, stress the value of soft skills like communication, teamwork, adaptability, and critical thinking. These skills are useful in AI-related jobs that require working with different people and collaborating with them.

**Stay Current and Encourage Lifelong Learning:** Tell kids to keep up with the latest developments in AI and related areas. Inspire an attitude of lifelong learning so that people can keep up with how AI is changing quickly.

Children can set themselves up for successful and important careers in AI by following these paths and getting the help and guidance they need.

**Conclusion:**

Using AI to its full potential in parenting and education.

In this book, we've talked about how Artificial Intelligence (AI) has the ability to change parenting and education. We set out on a journey to learn more about the AI revolution, its past, where it is now, and the many ways it is being used. AI has shown that it can change the way we raise children and teach in the modern world. It can help digital intelligence grow, open potential, keep children safe, and give teachers more power.

By using AI in how we raise our children, we open up a whole world of options. AI helps people get smarter, learn how to solve problems, and have more personalized learning experiences that fit their needs and hobbies. It encourages people to use their ideas, be creative, and try new things. This makes them well-rounded people who are ready to do well in a world that is becoming more and more digital. AI also gives us important information for early intervention, so we can keep better track of and study children's health and development milestones and take proactive steps when needed.

As parents and teachers, it's up to us to see AI's promise while also figuring out how to deal with its problems. In an AI-driven world, we need to be careful about how we use technology and take steps to protect our families' safety and privacy. Ethics are important, and we need to help our children develop ethical minds by teaching them to think critically and helping them understand the ethical effects of AI in everyday life. By having open and honest conversations about the moral limits of AI, we can help children use these tools in a way that is morally sound.

Looking ahead, we need to get ready for the future by looking into careers in AI and teaching our kids how to do well in this quickly changing area. To be ready for the future, we need to be willing to learn and change all the time. This will allow us to enjoy the benefits of AI while keeping our human values. We need to find a balance by teaching our kids about empathy, sensitivity, and privacy. We also need to remember that technology should be used to improve our lives and relationships, not replace them.

In conclusion, AI has the ability to change how parents and teachers do their jobs, but it's up to us to use its power in a good way. By using AI in our parenting and education systems, we can open up a whole new world of possibilities and build an environment that helps our kids reach their full potential. Let's take advantage of AI's benefits while keeping in mind its problems and social concerns. This way, we can create a future where AI and human values can live together in harmony, giving the next generation the tools they need to thrive in a digitally driven world.

# NURTURING THE FUTURE: EMBRACING AI RE-SPONSIBLY IN PARENTING

Nurturing the Future: How to Use AI in Parenting in a Responsible Way

In the last few pages of this book, we looked at the amazing ways AI could change parenting for the 21st century. We've seen how AI can personalize learning, help parents in smart ways, spot developmental needs, make things safer and more secure, and give emotional support and tools for mental health. AI is very powerful, and as we use it more, we must remember how important it is to use it in a responsible and decent way.

AI can help us be better parents, but it will never be able to take the place of human relationship and care. As parents, we need to find a good mix between using AI tools and having real, kind conversations with our kids. Technology should help us as parents by giving us useful information and resources, but it should never replace the love, care, and direction that only we, as parents, can give.

As we look to the future, we need to be aware of the problems and social questions that could come up because AI is developing so quickly. It is important to put data privacy first, make sure AI algo-rithms are clear, and think about the effects on society of depending too much on technology in parenting.

The AI revolution in parenting is just getting started, and as parents, teachers, and lawmakers, it's up to us to shape its path. We can use AI to help our kids and families if we use it in a responsible way, stay informed about what it can and can't do, and talk about it.

Let's end by remembering that the most important part of being a parent is the depth of our relationships, the strength of our bonds, and our unwavering commitment to our children's well-being. Let's use empathy, wisdom, and the unbreakable bond between a parent and a kid to guide us through the ever-changing world of AI.

Together, let's use the power of AI to change how we raise children in the modern world and make a future where technology and people can live together in peace to raise the next generation.

Thank you for joining us on this trip and may your path as a parent be full of love, joy, and endless possibilities.

# GLOSSARY OF KEY TERMS AND CONCEPTS FEATURED IN THE BOOK:

Glossary of key terms and concepts featured in the book:

**Artificial Intelligence (AI):** The field of computer science that focuses on creating intelligent machines capable of performing tasks that typically require human intelligence, such as learning, problem-solving, and decision-making.

**Personalized Learning:** An educational approach that tailors the learning experience to match an individual's unique needs, abilities, and preferences, often leveraging AI algorithms to adapt content and pace.

**Intelligent Tutoring Systems:** AI-powered educational systems that provide personalized instruction, feedback, and guidance to learners, adapting to their individual progress and optimizing learning outcomes.

**Virtual Assistants:** AI-based software programs that interact with users through voice or text, providing information, answering questions, and offering assistance on various topics, including parenting, child development, health, and nutrition.

**Developmental Delays:** A term used to describe when a child does not reach developmental milestones within the expected timeframe, often indicating potential challenges or difficulties in areas such as cognitive, motor, language, or social development.

**Computer Vision:** A branch of AI that focuses on enabling computers to understand and interpret visual information, allowing for tasks such as facial recognition, objects detection, and image analysis.

**Natural Language Processing (NLP):** A field of AI that involves the interaction between computers and human language, enabling machines to understand, interprets, and generates human language, facilitating tasks like language analysis and voice recognition.

**Smart Home Systems:** Technology-driven systems that automate and control various aspects of a home environment, including security, energy management, and safety features, often utilizing AI algorithms for enhanced functionality.

**Wearable Devices:** Technological devices that can be worn on the body, such as smartwatches or fitness trackers, often equipped with sensors and AI capabilities to monitor vital signs, activity levels, and location for improved safety and health tracking.

**Ethical Implementation:** The responsible and mindful use of AI technologies, considering factors such as privacy, data security, algorithmic bias, transparency, and accountability to ensure that AI systems are developed and deployed in a manner that aligns with ethical standards and societal well-being.

**Human Connection:** The deep emotional bond and meaningful interactions between parents and children, emphasizing the importance of nurturing relationships, empathy, and understanding, which should not be replaced or diminished by AI tools.

**Neural Networks:** Computing systems composed of interconnected nodes, or artificial neurons, inspired by the structure and functioning of biological neural networks. Neural networks are used in deep learning to process and learn from complex patterns in data.

**Robotics:** The field that combines AI, mechanical engineering, and computer science to develop machines or robots capable of performing tasks autonomously or with human-like capabilities, often with applications in areas such as caregiving or educational support.

**Internet of Things (IoT):** A network of interconnected physical devices or objects embedded with sensors, software, and connectivity, enabling them to collect and exchange data. IoT devices can enhance parenting through the integration of AI, such as smart home systems or wearable devices.

**Augmented Reality (AR) and Virtual Reality (VR):** Technologies that blend the virtual and physical worlds, providing immersive experiences or overlays of digital information onto the real environment. AR and VR can offer interactive and educational experiences for children, supported by AI algorithms.

**Parenting Strategies and Approaches:** Define terms that relate to different parenting styles or approaches, such as authoritative parenting, attachment parenting, positive parenting, or mindful parenting.

**Ethical Considerations:** Include terms that explore the ethical implications of AI in parenting, such as algorithmic bias, privacy concerns, data security, transparency, explain ability, and responsible AI governance.

**Child Development:** Define terms related to various aspects of child development, such as cognitive development, emotional intelligence, social skills, language acquisition, and motor skills.

**Mental Health and Well-being:** Define terms related to mental health, emotional well-being, and self-care for both children and parents, such as resilience, mindfulness, stress management, or self-regulation.

**Digital Citizenship and Online Safety:** Include terms that pertain to responsible digital usage, online safety, and fostering positive digital habits, such as cyberbullying, digital footprint, digital literacy, or digital well-being.

**Neuroscience and Brain Development:** Define terms related to the study of the brain and its development, such as neuroplasticity, synaptic pruning, executive functions, or brain-based learning.

**Related Technologies:**

**Machine Learning:** A subset of AI that focuses on developing algorithms and statistical models that enable computers to learn from and make predictions or decisions based on data, without being explicitly programmed.

**Deep Learning:** A specialized branch of machine learning that employs artificial neural networks, inspired by the structure and functions of the human brain, to process and learns from vast amounts of data, leading to more complex and advanced pattern recognition and decision-making capabilities.

**Natural Language Generation (NLG):** A technology that involves generating human-like language or text based on input data or instructions, allowing machines to produce written or spoken content that is coherent and contextually relevant.

**Computer Vision:** A field of AI that focuses on enabling computers to understand and interpret visual information from images or videos, mimicking human visual perception, and enabling tasks such as object recognition, image classification, and facial recognition.

**Reinforcement Learning:** A learning technique in which an AI agent learns to make decisions and take actions within an environment, receiving feedback or rewards for successful actions and adjusting its behavior through a process of trial and error.

**Natural Language Processing (NLP):** A branch of AI that involves the interaction between computers and human language, enabling machines to understand, interpret, and

# ACKNOWLEDGMENTS

Writing this book has been a life-changing experience full of times of inspiration, growth, and big insights. I'm grateful to everyone who has helped and led me along the way. Their help has been very important.

First and foremost, I want to thank my family from the bottom of my heart. Your constant love, support, and guidance have helped me get where I am today. Thank you for having faith in me and giving me the motivation to reach the stars.

I'd like to thank my friends and teachers for their wisdom, help, and interesting talks. Your ideas have helped me see things from a different angle and better understand what this book is about.

I'm very thankful to the people who study and were the first to work in Artificial Intelligence and education. Your ground-breaking work made it possible for the ideas in these pages to be possible. I'm grateful for the information you've given me and the progress you've made.

Thank you very much to the teachers and parents who have spent their lives shaping the minds of children. Your dedication, passion, and creative approaches to teaching have given me a lot to think about. Your stories and experiences have helped me find my way as I've been writing.

I want the people who read this book to know how much I appreciate them. Your openness to new ideas and perspectives and your desire to learn more are what make writing and sharing information so important. I hope that this book has given you some motivation and made you think about your own path.

Last but not least, I'd like to thank the people who worked on getting this book published. Your hard work, knowledge, and constant support have made this happen.

Thank you from the bottom of my heart to everyone who helped make this book and my own growth possible. Your contributions have made a big difference in my life and have made the words on these pages better.

Thank you.

Anant

For any questions, please write to us at the following addresses:

**admin@enlightenedanant.com**

**https://enlightenedanant.com**

# DISCLAIMER

This book, "Enlightened Parent's Guide in AI Education, " is written solely for the aim of enlightening and informing its readers. Ananat has taken great care to provide information that is both up-to-date and accurate. However, neither the author nor the publisher makes any guarantees or warranties, either stated or implied, as to the availability, accuracy, suitability, or completeness of the information, products, services, or related visuals presented in this book.

This book presents the author's research, experiences, and opinions on the subject matter. It is not meant to replace the services of a lawyer or doctor. Readers are urged to seek out the help of experts and professionals in the relevant fields for information that is specific to their own situations.

The author and publisher accept no responsibility for the accuracy, completeness, or usefulness of the information contained herein, or for any decisions made or actions taken in reliance thereon. Both the author and the publisher disclaim any and all liability for any loss, injury, or damage that might occur as a result of using the information presented herein.

This book does not support or guarantee the quality, trustworthiness, or safety of the products, services, or information supplied by any external sources to which it links, references, or recommends. Readers should exercise caution and good judgment when interacting with any outside resources.

# CONGRATULATIONS

Parents Now that you have the knowledge and wisdom to nurture your child's mind, body, and soul, as well as to embrace the possibilities that AI brings while maintaining a healthy balance with their wellbeing and morals, you are torchbearers of illumination.

The use of AI has the potential to completely transform the way we learn, think, and create, as you have seen throughout this book. But let's not lose sight of the fact that your unfailing love and support are the most effective transformation agent. The human touch is what will give AI its potential life and turn it into a positive force in the world.

Do not forget the importance of balance in all sides of life, dear parents. Although AI can boost productivity and efficiency, it is vital to place a priority on spending quality time with your child, fostering emotional intelligence, and making genuine relationships.

May the future of your child be filled with wisdom, goodness, and limitless opportunities.

I wish you and your child a life full of happiness and enlightenment.

Heartfelt regards, Anant